COMMUNICATE
OR ELSE

ENDORSEMENTS

Scott Danner
Freedom Street Partners
If you are looking for an effective strategy to nurture client relationships and open relationships with prospects, this book is for you. Communicate or Else is a great guide to help you leverage your unique voice with your audience.

Michele Nettesheim
Phoenix Wealth Advisors
Communicate or Else is an invaluable tool for financial advisers who want to attract new clients (and keep their current clients happy) without compromising their own style and values. Tim understands that getting a ton of prospect calls is meaningless (and a waste of precious time) if the prospects aren't a good fit for your practice.

Rick Fisher
Fisher Wealth Management
This book is an easy and must read for any financial advisor looking to serve people through better communication. Business is a contact sport. These ideas around embracing technology to leverage your time will provide value to anyone who gives it an honest try. Well done!

Randy Brunson
Centurion Advisors Group
Tim has mastered the art of communicating with clients and prospects. He understands the need to continuously build awareness and credibility, and the value in sharing professional expertise on a consistent basis. I recommend this book as a "must-have' resource for the financial professional.

Chad Rushing
Freedom Street Partners
Incorporating Tim's simple action plan has completely changed the way I communicate and build relationships. Now that video and direct email marketing is part of my process, I get a personal thank you from clients on almost everything that is produced. It has become much more important to my business than I ever anticipated. After 30 years in the business, I didn't realize that my blind spot was right in front of me.

Steve Ford
Artisan Wealth Advisors
Tim defines effective marketing as excellent communication to build and nurture relationships. If financial advisors are primarily in the relationship business, then the concepts in this book are critical. Tim will challenge you to rethink how you communicate to your audience. His book is packed with practical ideas to help you build and nurture relationships.

Rusty Bacon
Paraclete
Communicate or Else is a very practical and easy to follow guide to effectively communicating with not just clients, but also prospects. In an industry where advisors typically default to pre-packaged, generic content, Tim skillfully explains how an advisor can gain a "voice" and become a "thought leader" - not just throw mud at a wall when it comes to marketing. This step-by-step guide provides the tools necessary for an advisor to reflect on their true value proposition and passions and leverage those differentiators into a systematic communication campaign that grows their business. Tim clearly has a command on the space, and I recommend this book for any advisor looking to modernize their marketing and gain new clients.

Margie Wiley
Freedom Street Partners
Tim has a unique way of making marketing seem less threatening to a business owner. As business owners we feel that we do a great job telling people about what we do, but often we find that the words do not always reflect the services we offer. I value that Tim can take what is in my brain and put it into words that reflect my values and personality. Clear communication to my clients and prospects is a key foundation to our business.

Terry Wiles
Stonegate Financial
Tim Riddle's *Communicate or Else* is an outstanding guide to help any financial advisor. I especially feel this is a great read for that advisor that never seems to find the time to elevate their business to the next level. I particularly believe that marketing is a marathon and not a sprint!

Chris Edgcomb
Edgcomb Advisors
Communicate or Else is a blueprint for marketing success. It is a simple, straight-forward guide for advisors that want to communicate their value to the clients they *want* to work with.

Tim Portelance
Freedom Street Partners
Tim's simple marketing strategies helped me effectively maintain targeted communication with both clients and prospects. The videos, in particular, allowed my personality to come through enabling me to strengthen relationships in a consistent manor that was insightful and educational but not salesy.

Tom Domin
From a personal standpoint, applying the principles of this book has given me perspective on how to thoughtfully scale communication with my clients and target audience. I knew from the time I applied these principles it would be a "reap what

you sow" type of environment. At the time of writing this, I am just shy of one year of working with Tim and the Discover Blind Spots team and my practice has grown by nearly 70% with a large portion attributable to the nurture campaigns and communication I have created through the strategies of this book.

If you are willing to put in the work required and have a defined target audience, I think you owe it to yourself and your clients to find a way to integrate the principles found in *Communicate or Else*.

Mark Kemp
Kemp Harvest Financial Group
Tim's book is awesome. It emphasizes the importance of communication along with building genuine relationships; it just makes sense!

For the past two years, I've worked with Tim & his team to communicate with our existing clients and fuel referrals to new clients.

Read the book, learn from the book, embrace the book, and implement the book's principles. They're a go.

COMMUNICATE OR ELSE

A New Perspective on Marketing for
Financial Advisors

TIM RIDDLE

PALMETTO
PUBLISHING
Charleston, SC
www.PalmettoPublishing.com

Communicate Or Else
Copyright © 2023 by Tim Riddle

All rights reserved

Hardcover ISBN: 979-8-8229-2064-4
Paperback ISBN: 979-8-8229-2065-1
eBook ISBN: 979-8-8229-2066-8

DEDICATION

To my wife Stacy - you make me believe I can do anything. My dreams have never been too big for you. In fact, you believe them before I do. Thanks for always being there and the first person I trust to read anything I write. I love you. Thanks for loving me.

To Fletcher and Carly - two people I am honored to call my children and teammates at Discover Blinds Spots. It is one of God's greatest blessings to work with both of you.

To our team at Discover Blind Spots - thanks for serving so faithfully to help our clients communicate effectively. I am in awe of your talents. Thanks for sharing them.

To our clients of Discover Blind Spots - we are blessed to love you as people first and clients second. I am humbled by the opportunity to serve each of you.

TABLE OF CONTENTS

Introduction ·1

Part 1 ·7
Chapter 1   Marketing Confusion · · · · · · · · · · · · · · · ·9
Chapter 2   Common Marketing Blind Spots · · · · · · · · · ·15
Chapter 3   A New Perspective on Marketing · · · · · · · · ·23
Chapter 4   The Value of Clear Communication · · · · · · · ·31
Chapter 5   Values to Consider for Your Marketing
              Foundation ·37

Part 2 ·45
Chapter 6   What's Your Marketing Personality? · · · · · · · ·47
Chapter 7   Defining Your 10 Percent · · · · · · · · · · · · · ·51
Chapter 8   Defining Your Audience · · · · · · · · · · · · · · ·57
Chapter 9   Defining Your Rhythm · · · · · · · · · · · · · · · ·63
Chapter 10   Who Will Communicate to Whom? · · · · · · · ·69
Chapter 11   Content: Where Do I Start? · · · · · · · · · · · · ·73

Part 3 ·79
Chapter 12   Before You Get Started · · · · · · · · · · · · · · · ·81
Chapter 13   Using Automation · · · · · · · · · · · · · · · · · · ·85
Chapter 14   Email Is Not Dead · · · · · · · · · · · · · · · · · · ·91
Chapter 15   How to Use Video · · · · · · · · · · · · · · · · · ·101

Chapter 16 Becoming a Thought Leader · · · · · · · · · · · · 109

Chapter 17 How to Create a Website That Is Not an
Art Museum · 117

Chapter 18 Let's Get Real About Social Media · · · · · · · · 125

Chapter 19 A Marketing Calendar to Consider · · · · · · · · 131

Conclusion · **139**

INTRODUCTION

The year was 1996. I had started a textile company in 1991, manufacturing specialty products for the gift and home fashion industry. Five years later, we experienced tremendous growth; we had $13 million in sales, a few thousand accounts, and close to 100 employees.

On this particular day, I purchased a teleprompter for our VP of sales. I wanted him to record videos to better communicate with our independent sales reps who lived all over the U.S. I admit our team thought I had lost my mind.

First, video was still very new and only being used by cutting-edge companies. The only way to share videos universally was to save them on large floppy discs and send them through the mail. I know, I'm dating myself.

I remember being asked, "Tim, a teleprompter…really?" Only news anchors used teleprompters back then, and they were large boxes that cost thousands of dollars.

I guess that's my first introduction to marketing. Although I'm not sure I understood that it was marketing. I often used "marketing and sales" in the same sentence, so I assumed they were the same.

The bottom line: I wanted to grow our sales, which started with our independent sales reps. Independent meant they sold our products along with products from other companies. My idea: communicate with each of them in a creative and compelling way so we could be first out of their bag of products as opposed to last. If we could communicate better and more often, they might be motivated to talk about us to current and potential customers.

Fast forward 21 years. It's now 2017, and I am the executive pastor of a large church I attended and served for many years. After an invitation from the senior pastor to use my marketplace skills for a different purpose, I decided to leave the marketplace and join this team.

I was asked to lead a new $2.5 million capital campaign for a building expansion. As we were dreaming about communicating the vision, I thought of two words: What if? So I wrote those two words on sticky notes and randomly placed them throughout the church office. I wanted to create interest and intrigue. I also wanted to challenge our team to think differently. I wanted to change their perspective on the challenges of a capital campaign. This was another experience with marketing in my career, although I still can't say that I understood the meaning. Once again, I just wanted to communicate creatively.

Fast forward a few more years, and I had just started my new business, Discover Blind Spots. The name was inspired by a book I co-wrote: *Blind Spots, What You Don't See Can Hurt You.*

It was a beautiful Friday afternoon, and I called a good friend to see if he wanted to go for a bike ride. We have ridden thousands of miles together over the years. We often talked about life, family, and business during those rides.

My friend is a financial advisor, and as we slowly pedaled to warm up, I asked this question: "Hey Jeff, how do you nurture relationships with your clients?"

He gave me a puzzled look as if to say, "I don't understand," but he humored me with a reply. He said, "I meet with them or take them to lunch periodically."

I asked, "How many clients do you have in your database?"

He said, "Around 300 or so."

I then asked, "How many lunches did you have last year?"

That's when he smiled and said, "Obviously, not that many."

I then said, "What if I could provide a way for you to communicate using *your* voice to *your* audience without using canned content to help nurture those relationships?"

Jeff said, "I'm in!"

After all, there was no way Jeff would have time to meet face-to-face with every client as often as he wanted to. Jeff has a very successful business and cares deeply for his clients. So his lack of meeting one-on-one was not a matter of want, but time.

Now fast forward two years later, and I met Bill, another successful financial advisor. Bill said, "Hey, Tim, I have a problem. I have a thousand prospects in my database."

I said, "That doesn't sound like a problem!"

Bill explained that closing those prospects was not a problem when they were ready, but he didn't have an effective follow-up plan for those just "kicking the tires." He relied on his memory to reach out periodically, but his plan was not practical or sustainable. I asked Bill, "What if I could provide a way to communicate using *your* voice to *your* audience to nurture those prospects to keep *you* top of mind?"

Bill said, "I'm in!"

That's when my idea of marketing began to take shape. But not just any marketing—a different approach: a marketing approach focused more on building relationships than sales, although it would eventually lead to the same destination. I wanted to develop a marketing approach focused on excellent communication rather than a great sales pitch. I wanted a marketing strategy allowing you to sell without being salesy.

Hence, I started my new company, Discover Blind Spots, to help financial advisors solve this problem: How do you use *your* voice to communicate to *your* audience to develop and nurture relationships with clients and prospects?

And that's what this book is about: a new perspective on marketing for financial advisors.

But before I end this section, let me tell you what it's not about. First, it's not a get-rich-quick scheme. Unlike many of the enticing offers you see on social media, I'm not promising that you'll triple your business in three months.

However, it is a sustainable and effective plan that will help you nurture your relationships with clients and prospects. It is a plan that will make it easy for your clients to talk about you to others, and prospects will feel like they know the character of who you are before your first meeting.

It is a short book. That is intentional and strategic. Many advisors don't have time to sit and read for hours in today's busy world. You should be able to read this book in about two hours.

This book is also practical. It is based on this simple principle: Relationships improve with excellent communication. Before you finish reading, you will have several practical strategies you can implement immediately.

Over the past several years, I have worked primarily with financial advisors. This book culminates all the experience and research I have gained from those relationships. If you are not a financial advisor, that's OK. If you genuinely care about building relationships with your clients and prospects, this book's principles will also apply to you.

And finally, the book is strategically laid out in three sections:

1. Marketing, a new perspective. I need to share the reason for my view of marketing to give you context for the rest of the book; whether you agree or not is up to you.

2. Designing *your* marketing strategy. Your strategy should align with *you*. Aligning your strategy with who you are is critical to sustainability. I don't want to present a one-size-fits-all marketing plan. Instead, I want to help you make sure the marketing clothes you wear fit you well!

3. Best practices you can start applying today. You may be tempted to jump to this section, but don't. If you don't clearly understand the "why," you will be frustrated with the "how."

Now, let's get started!

PART 1

Foundations provide the stability for many large structures. Although this book is not a large structure, it is my hope that it doesn't become a paperweight or collect dust in the corner of your office. Marketing strategies can change from time to time, but the core *foundational* principles remain the same. In this section, I want to share some of those principles from a new perspective that inspired this book. Let's start with why! Once you understand the *why,* I believe you will find more value in the *how.*

CHAPTER 1

MARKETING CONFUSION

I was excited about a presentation I was about to make to a potential new client. I had worked hard to pull together just the right pitch: not too much, not too little. I had worked extra hard to be clear and eliminate insider language and marketing terms that nobody would understand.

The pitch seemed to be going well. At least, I noticed a lot of smiles as I was talking. When I finished, I asked for questions, and one person said, "So basically, you create content for our social media?" The confusing part of that question was that I never mentioned social media in my pitch. That's when it hit me that their perception of marketing was totally different from mine.

Another time, I was sitting in a large conference room, and at the end of my presentation, someone asked, "So what's an email campaign?" I stopped and realized that their understanding of marketing was minimal, which was OK, but shame on me for not being clear.

Another time I finished a pitch and was asked, "So when do we get started on the website?" Their idea of marketing was focused on website creation.

So what is marketing, after all?

I recently Googled the word "marketing," and I received 7.2 billion results. Today it's probably more. And guess what. They are not all saying the same thing. No wonder there is confusion.

Identify the Audience

First, you must identify your audience to find the correct answer. Unfortunately, most people miss this part. Many quick-fix schemes on social media focus on a transactional audience. Very few focus on building relationships instead of just followers.

For example, be cautious if you read about a snazzy plan that will triple your business in ninety days. In my experience, I've not seen any of these work for building long-term relationships. Of course, I'm not suggesting that the claim of tripling their business was false, but I doubt it was solely because of a slick ninety-day marketing strategy. And if it was, implementing the strategy in a relationship business might not be as easy as you think.

Building Relationships

Another perception of marketing is trying to attach it to sales. Yes, they are related, but they are distant cousins, not brother and sister. Marketing can and should lead to sales, but marketing can also help you keep the sales you have. I'll talk more about that in Chapter 3.

Marketing for financial advisors is a chance to grow relationships. If you are an advisor, you are not a transactional business, although you handle many transactions. Most great relationships are built over time. It takes time to nurture and grow a relationship. You probably do that by meeting face-to-face, but your marketing reinforces those face-to-face meetings. Your actions and words need to align.

For example, I recently received a marketing email from a famous marketer I know and follow. The email was personal and well-written. I thought he was writing just to me. I was flattered. He included a call to action stating that he wanted to connect with me and encouraged me to reply to the email. I quickly started typing a response.

Before hitting send, I noticed my reply was addressed to info@hiscompanyname. At that point, I realized I was just one of many he sent this email to. I quickly deleted my reply before sending it. I felt duped. Not that his tactics were wrong—I'm sure they were successful for him—but it was a transactional strategy pretending to be relational.

Precursor to Sales
For a financial advisor, I view marketing as the precursor to sales. Your marketing is the sowing of seeds, and sales are the harvest. And the last time I checked, the farmer doesn't plant today and harvest tomorrow. There is a season of planting and nurturing if you want to reap the best harvest.

Recently, I received a request to connect through LinkedIn. I have noticed a trend lately, and I wondered how long it would take to receive a message asking for my business. I didn't have to wait long: three minutes! I guess this marketing strategy works for some people, but not for me and not for many financial advisors I work with.

Another way to view marketing is that it can help you earn the right to meet with a prospect or move a client to a deeper relationship. In essence, prospects and clients gain respect for you over time. As your message starts to sink in, cold prospects become warm and warm clients become even warmer, possibly leading to new business from both. Bottom line: It takes time, and those who view it as a marathon, not a sprint, are finding success.

Here's another confusion. Your marketing doesn't replace face-to-face meetings with clients and prospects. I've heard advisors say, "I really need your help with marketing because I want to reduce the one-on-one time I have to spend with clients." Spoiler alert! Great marketing doesn't replace your current relational strategy; it supports and enhances it. It allows you to nurture relationships virtually in addition to those face-to-face meetings.

CONCLUSION

As you are tempted to buy a new marketing course or copy a strategy from someone claiming success, don't forget to ask, "Is this a transactional or relational strategy?" You only have one chance to make a first impression. Don't allow your marketing to create the wrong one.

CHAPTER 2

COMMON MARKETING BLIND SPOTS

Throughout my career, I've experienced great joy when I've helped someone uncover a blind spot. On the other hand, I've experienced great sadness when I can't. Sometimes, removing a blind spot can be painful; other times, it can be enlightening.

In 2018, I co-authored a book entitled *Blind Spots: What You Don't See Can Hurt You*. It's a faith-based book that focuses on uncovering and eliminating blind spots so we can live our best lives. Also, it inspired me to start my current company, Discover Blind Spots.

Discover Blind Spots is a marketing company that works with financial advisors. So what's the connecting thread?

Our blind spots keep us from being our best. In essence, they limit our abilities to accomplish what we set out to do. Blind spots in marketing are usually caused by doing the same thing over and over, expecting a different result. That's also called insanity!

Removing a blind spot can change your perspective and your scenery. For example, we experience one view when we walk out of the front door of our home and look around the neighborhood. But if we climb on the roof of our home, we will experience a totally different view. So let's climb on the roof for a different perspective to uncover a few potential marketing blind spots for financial advisors.

Newsletters

Newsletters are one of the primary marketing tools for many advisors. But newsletters are different from what they used to be. Typically, they are low-priority in today's busy world.

For example, I follow a few companies that I love. I have provided my email address so these companies can stay in touch with me. If I ever receive a newsletter, my first impression is: "Low priority. I'll read it when I have time." Usually, the email sits in my email inbox for a few days even though I have every intention of reading it, which usually never happens. Eventually, I move it to a folder to review later, which also never seems to happen.

Let's face it: Newsletters are a lot of work. You only have so much time to dedicate to marketing. The question is whether a newsletter produces enough results to warrant the energy. If it does, keep doing it. If it doesn't, reevaluate!

Website

A website is a great marketing tool. However, you should not put all your marketing eggs in your website basket. A familiar blind spot is a perception that once the website is complete, so is your marketing.

Consider your website a door your audience can enter to learn more about your business. Most prospects who view your website for the first time are not ready to engage at that moment. It's as if they are driving by your building but need more time to walk through your front door. If your website is your sole marketing tool, many prospects will drive by, take a look, and keep driving. Unless you support your website with additional strategies to communicate your message, your website will eventually become a white elephant, and you will be forgotten—more on this in Part 3 of this book.

Canned Content

Often, I hear advisors say, "I get all my marketing from corporate." Others will say, "I subscribe to this or that service for my content." The blind spot is the assumption that canned content is "good enough."

In today's noisy world, there are multiple voices that your clients and prospects can listen to. The problem with canned content is that it's not your voice. Yes, your clients and prospects might find value in an article you pass along occasionally, but usually, they want to hear from *you*. For example, they may think, "This is great information, but I want to know what *you* think." So don't hit the easy button. Instead, start sharing *your* voice with *your* audience.

Email Is Dead—It's All About Social Media

No one will deny that social media has changed the marketing landscape. You can't scroll without seeing an ad promising to triple your business in three easy steps. It has provided an easy stage to share products and services. The problem with a social media stage is that you typically speak to a passive audience rather than an active one. Passive because the audience is usually scrolling through their feed randomly, killing time, and not actively leaning in to engage.

Email, on the other hand, is a communication from one person to another person. Sure, marketing emails are usually sent to a larger group. Still, if you use automation well and your content is engaging, your audience has a better chance of feeling that you are speaking directly to them—more on this in Chapters 13 and 14.

Here's a question to consider. What percentage of social media posts do you read daily compared with the number of posts available to read? That percentage is probably small. Now, how many emails do you receive each day that you at least look at the subject line? My guess is a much higher percentage.

So email is not dead. It is still the number one marketing tool you have. It also allows you to communicate with whom you want, when you want, and with the message you want. You decide.

Social media is a communication platform you rent and play by someone else's rules, and those rules often change. Social media has its purpose and can help share your message, but don't focus solely on social media and expect meaningful engagement—more on this in Chapter 18.

I Don't Need Marketing, I Only Focus on Clients

When I hear this comment, I usually ask, "So you don't need to communicate with clients?" If great marketing is about building relationships (more on this in Chapter 3), your communication with clients is as critical as it is for prospects.

Most financial advisors don't experience a lot of churn. As their book of business grows to an acceptable level to provide the income they desire, there can be a tendency to sit back and assume that marketing is solely for advisors looking for new prospects.

Research shows that 65 percent of clients who leave do so because of indifference. They feel you don't pay enough attention to them. Yet who has enough time to meet face-to-face with every client monthly? Your marketing communication can help close the indifference gap. Clients will stay with you through good and bad times as long as they consistently hear your voice.

It's Too Complicated

I agree that today's marketing world is confusing. There are tons of strategies to choose from. Often, we default to the strategy of throwing things against the wall to see if something sticks. This blind spot often leads to impatience and the unwillingness to stick around long enough to see whether the strategy works. Before we know it, we default to a start-and-stop strategy that creates confusion and frustration for you and your team.

CONCLUSION

Here's a final thought about blind spots. Too often, we assume that a blind spot indicates we are doing something wrong, and the energy to do it right feels overwhelming.

Over my career, I have been pleasantly surprised to uncover blind spots that don't require a radical change but a minor tweak. For example, maybe 90 percent of your marketing strategy is perfect, but 10 percent needs a slight tweak to make the 90 percent excel.

My intention with this chapter is not to point out mistakes but to offer a different perspective that might not be as overwhelming as you think. Depending on where you are on your journey, perhaps this book will affirm many of your current strategies and allow you to adjust or add the small pieces you are missing.

CHAPTER 3

A NEW PERSPECTIVE ON MARKETING

I attended a financial advisor conference several years ago where Dr. Henry Cloud was a keynote speaker. Dr. Cloud is a renowned author, speaker, counselor, and coach. I'd heard him speak in other settings and was curious to hear his message to a room full of financial advisors.

He started his talk by saying he wanted to focus on two R's significant for every financial advisor. He then said that the first R was evident, so he would only spend a bit of his time on it. However, the second R was often overlooked, and that's where he would focus most of his talk.

The first R was "results." Dr. Cloud said that financial advisors must achieve results for their clients. That's obvious. Your job is to help a client plan and grow their portfolio over time.

Then Dr. Cloud moved to the second R, "relationships." He said that as a successful financial advisor, you must be intentional about growing relationships with clients and prospects. However, that intentionality might be more challenging than you think.

As a financial advisor, you probably don't meet with every client monthly. Most clients don't have the time to do that anyway. However, the gaps between meetings can cause indifference in a relationship.

As I stated in Chapter 1, if you Google the word "marketing," you will see billions of results to comb through, and you can count on a bit of confusion if you decide to look at a few of them. Why? Because not everyone is saying the same thing.

Let me simplify and provide a new perspective for marketing, especially if you care about the second R Dr. Cloud spoke about.

Communication Builds Relationships

At the core of all marketing is excellent communication, and excellent communication leads to great relationships. Looking back over my years as a business owner, leader, husband, parent, mentor, and friend, the quality of my relationships required great communication. I often refer to the two C's: clarity and consistency. If your communication is clear and consistent, your relationships will grow. However, when I peel back the layers of relationships that have struggled occasionally, unclear and infrequent communication is always part of the issue.

Marketing Does Not Equal Sales

Now, let's clarify one critical blind spot before moving forward. Marketing is *not* sales. We often hear the words mentioned in the same sentence as if they are interchangeable—marketing and sales, sales and marketing. Yes, marketing should lead to sales, just like excellent communication should lead to better relationships, but marketing is the precursor to sales. Remember, marketing is the planting, and sales are the harvest.

Planting and harvesting don't happen simultaneously. The planting requires a season of nurturing before you can enjoy the harvest. Also, it is often hard to directly connect the outcome of a specific sale to your marketing content in a relationship business, which leads to my next point.

Don't try to implement a transactional marketing strategy in a relationship business. Every week, I receive canned emails trying to sell me something. The most humorous are those that want to sell me a marketing service to grow my marketing business. Others claim they have spent countless hours researching me and feel I am a perfect candidate to purchase a fast food franchise. I have nothing against fast food, but I've never thought about opening a franchise.

Here's the problem. Cold emails are OK, although they are certainly not my preference. Asking for the sale in a cold email is like asking my wife to marry me on the first date. My wife, Stacy and I, dated for three years before the relationship was ready for a proposal! It took lots of excellent communication over those three years to get to that point. Of course, I'm not suggesting you wait three years before you ask for the sale, but you get my point.

If marketing is planting, take time to nurture the field you are planting in. I love this quote from Ralph Waldo Emerson: "Who you are speaks so loudly, I can't hear a word you are saying." Make sure your audience knows a bit about who you are before you propose.

Who Is Your Audience?

Next, let's talk about your audience. In the spirit of simplification, your audience consists of two groups: clients and prospects. Although your message for both can be similar, the purpose of your communication is different.

You communicate with prospects to open the relationship to close the sale. You communicate with clients to nurture the relationship to keep the sale.

Let's start with clients. As mentioned in the previous Chapter, you market to clients to prevent indifference. Silence invites a client to draw conclusions about your relationship that might not be true. Remember, great communication leads to great relationships, and you never want to defer your communication to the mainstream media, especially in a volatile market.

First, you communicate with clients to remind them why they work with you. Casting and recasting that vision is critical. I've told my wife, Stacy, how much I love and appreciate her thousands of times. I doubt we would still be married for

38 years if I'd stopped sharing those words the day after our wedding.

Next, you should market to your clients so they will talk about you. Referrals are a critical part of your business, as you know. According to one source, 95 percent of new business comes from referrals from existing clients. But don't default to the old way of referrals. For example, refrain from asking clients to introduce you to their friends. Nobody wants to do that.

Instead, use your marketing to clarify the vision for what you do, the problems you solve, and the services you provide. Also, use your marketing to share your voice as a thought leader. We will talk more specifically about how to do that in Chapter 16.

Give your clients a reason to share with their friends and family the great work you do. For example, your happily married clients might know someone recently divorced. So if you share your thoughts about putting your life back together financially after a divorce, it would make sense for those clients to refer their divorced friends to you. Provide content to your clients that inspires them to share it as a solution for others. A warm referral is always better than a cold one.

Now let's move to prospects. Again, patience is essential before you propose to a prospect, especially a cold one. You must warm the relationship before earning the right to have the "becoming a client" conversation. Your marketing content to a prospect will allow them to date you before they decide to marry you. The speed of the dating correlates with the temperature of the relationship. If they are a referral and already warm, perhaps you can rush to the altar.

One strategy I love is offering content to a prospect that is helpful to them whether they do business with you or not. I often recommend saying that up front. I know an advisor who, after talking to a prospect who is not ready to become a client, will say: "I have some great content that will be helpful to you whether you decide to become a client or not. I would love to send it to you from time to time."

Prospects agree to receive his content nearly 100 percent of the time. And this advisor can be sure that when the time is right, he will remain top of mind for this prospect and most likely close the sale at some point.

Let's face it, this marketing strategy for prospects is much better than writing their names down and calling them every few months to see whether they are ready to become clients. Instead, be patient, and be willing to "date" for a while to earn the right to become their financial advisor when they are ready.

CONCLUSION

One of the hardest things to identify with a marketing strategy is the return on investment. Throughout my years, I have had several conversations in which a client wanted to attach a dollar return for every dollar spent on marketing. I get it. Your marketing needs to get results—after all, that's the first R Dr. Cloud discussed. However, always remember to measure the right results with patience.

Marketing dollars this year might not lead to a harvest until next year. Often, it takes time and consistency for a message to resonate and lead to results. It takes time for your clients to internalize your message and share it. It takes time for prospects to feel comfortable enough to share their financial imperfections.

Remember the words of Theodore Roosevelt: "People don't care how much you know until they know how much you care." You can show how much you know rather quickly, but showing how much you care takes time.

CHAPTER 4:
THE VALUE OF CLEAR COMMUNICATION

I was sitting in a room with a leadership team I was part of. I was sharing a sensitive topic and trying to be as clear as possible. When the meeting ended, I noticed tension in the room. Over the next week, I continued to feel the tension. My first reaction was confusion, which led to frustration at the group's reaction.

After a week or two, we decided to get back together to clarify the previous conversation. So I wouldn't feel defensive, I asked the members of the group to share their concerns. When the first person started to restate the conversation, I noticed some inconsistencies in what I supposedly said—or at least what I thought I said. I patiently waited until they finished, and I began to clarify. I said, "Thanks for sharing your thoughts, but when you mentioned (specific topic), I didn't say that." At that point, the entire group said, "Yes, you did."

Bottom line, whether I said it or not, that's what the group heard. My communication was not as clear as I thought.

If clarity is essential when sitting in the same room, it is even more critical when sending marketing content to clients and prospects. That's perhaps one of the most significant issues with marketing content: It's not clear.

The Curse of Knowledge

Many financial advisors allow their marketing to fall victim to the curse of knowledge. Knowledge is helpful, but too much knowledge can lead to confusion.

I love what Dan and Chip Heath write in their book *Made to Stick: Why Some Ideas Survive and Others Die*: "Once we know something, we find it hard to imagine what it was like not to know it. Our knowledge has cursed us."

They write about a 1990 experiment by Elizabeth Newton, a PhD student at Stanford. The experiment was called "tappers" vs. "listeners." Tappers were given a list of very familiar songs, such as "Happy Birthday" and "The Star-Spangled Banner." They were asked to "tap" them out to see if the listener could identify the tune. Before the experiment, the tappers were asked the odds that the listeners would guess correctly. They predicted 50 percent. The results: 2.5 percent! The authors go on to say that when a tapper taps, you hear the song in your head. Go ahead and try it now. However, a listener can't always hear the same song; they often only hear a bunch of disconnected taps, like random Morse Code.

So how do we avoid the curse of knowledge? How can we ensure our audience hears the same tune we are singing?

KISS

First, keep it simple. Many of today's writing apps will grade the clarity of your content, and I find it interesting that the benchmark reader is usually an elementary-grade student.

The acronym KISS is a familiar one: Keep it simple, stupid. The term was first used in the US Navy and is thought to have been coined by Kelly Johnson, the lead engineer at the Lockheed Skunk Works corporation. Johnson told the team at Lockheed that their designs should be simple enough to be repaired by someone in a combat situation with only basic mechanical training. He felt that their products would cost lives and quickly become obsolete if they weren't simple and easy to understand.

In the marketing world, your audience will quickly abandon a complex message. It's not that they don't have the intelligence to understand it; they don't have the time. Your message is competing with every other message they receive. Simplicity will win the battle more often than not.

Many times, we assume that keeping things complex makes them appear more valuable. But we need to recognize the potential blind spot that keeping things complex might make us *feel* more valuable. Don't allow your insecurity to cause you to complicate your message. I recently heard a podcast host say, "Complexity and insecurity are kissing cousins." Don't be a complexifier; be a simplifier.

How to Be a Simplifier

When you create your marketing content, simplify it into three sections. First, introduce the topic or concept, drawing attention to the pain point it creates. Usually, that pain point is anxiety or confusion. If your marketing content doesn't address a pain point, it probably falls in the "information" category. As a financial advisor, you must communicate information occasionally, but don't let it monopolize your marketing content. If you focus solely on communicating information, the curse of knowledge may tempt you. Clients do business with you mostly for one reason: you have a solution to a problem or pain point they have. The sooner you can speak to that problem, the quicker your audience will engage.

Second, provide a few helpful tips to address the problem or pain point. Notice I said a few helpful tips. Recently I had an advisor want to create a piece of marketing content listing a hundred tips to solve a specific problem. Although I love their enthusiasm, I doubt their audience will value it as much. Often, we think that the more tips we provide, the more tips our audience will remember. For example, why not provide a hundred tips in hopes that they remember twenty-five? Isn't that better than offering only three or four with the potential of remembering only one or two? The problem with complexity is that there is a tipping point. If you hand me three bags full of groceries, I can probably carry them to the car. But if you keep piling on the bags, eventually, I will drop all of them. In this example, retention is zero. Be careful not to cause your audience to "drop the bags" because of providing too many tips.

Finally, end with an invitation to talk more about how this pain point affects your audience's specific situation. Your marketing should lead to a continued conversation with a client or a new conversation with a prospect. As a financial advisor, you can't close the sale with marketing; it can only get your audience in front of you for a face-to-face conversation. The win is not the sale; the win is that your marketing can lead to a conversation to grow the relationship.

CONCLUSION

I love the story from James W. Moore's *When All Else Fails…
Read the Instructions* about a four-year-old boy who was in the
back seat of the family car, eating an apple. "Daddy," said the
child, "why is my apple turning brown?" His father explained,
"Because after you ate the outer skin off, the meat of the apple
came into contact with the air, which caused it to oxidize,
changing its molecular structure, and thus turning it into a
different color." There was a long silence, and the little boy
asked softly, "Daddy, are you talking to me?"

Clients and prospects already understand the complexity of what you do. That's why they reach out to you for help.
They hope you can simplify their lives, not complicate them
with financial jargon. And making complex things simple is
not that simple. Take the time to create content that doesn't
leave your audience wondering whether you are still talking
to them.

CHAPTER 5

VALUES TO CONSIDER FOR YOUR MARKETING FOUNDATION

I love to talk about values. In fact, I'd rather focus on values than spout off a fancy mission or vision statement. Why? Because values determine how you live your life. If you let them, they will hold you accountable.

At Discover Blind Spots, our values are:

- Highly responsive
- Incredibly kind
- Overly generous
- Pursuing excellence

Although our strategies might change occasionally, our values remain the same—and they influence those changing strategies.

So what does this have to do with marketing?

It's important to define your marketing values too. If not, you will find yourself constantly in a reactive state instead of a proactive one.

Although I don't believe any marketing strategy is one size fits all, there are core marketing values you should embrace to keep you on a proactive path.

Consistency

Embracing the value of consistency is vital for every marketing strategy. Marketing is a marathon, not a sprint. Slow and steady wins the race more often than not.

The rule of seven is prevalent in most marketing strategies. The rule states that a prospect needs to hear a consistent message seven times before they will take action and respond. Consistency is critical in both the message and rhythm of delivery. If you are not careful, your message can drift. Often, we get bored with our marketing message and decide to change it. Other times, we get too excited about our message and create content at a pace that is not sustainable. Lots of changing messages followed by long periods of silence because you ran out of gas will leave you frustrated and your audience confused.

Clarity

All content we consume requires our brains to engage at some level to understand. Remember that your content competes with lots of noise in the world—our brains long for clarity, not complexity. Your audience will gravitate to clear content that is easy to consume over content that requires too much brain energy. Clear and easy has nothing to do with intelligence, only time. One of the greatest gifts you can give someone is to communicate with clarity to minimize the time of consumption.

Also, remember that clarity trumps being cute and clever. Refrain from thinking that a cute and clever cryptic message will engage your audience. Remember the New Coke ad campaign? It was one of history's biggest marketing blunders because it confused its audience.

Conciseness

Over my career, I have had many opportunities to communicate with various audiences. One form of communication is speaking. Each time I prepare a talk for a live audience, I remember a tip I heard about a great speech: "Create a great opening and a great closing and put them as close together as possible!" Many times, we are amazed at a speaker who can talk for hours. Actually, that's pretty easy. The hard part is reducing the same talk to ten minutes!

Being concise takes work. As John Maeda explains in *The Laws of Simplicity*, when President Woodrow Wilson was asked how long it took him to prepare his speeches, he responded: "That depends on the length of the speech. If it is a ten-minute speech, it takes me all of two weeks to prepare it; if it is a half hour speech, it takes me a week; if I can talk as long as I want to, it requires no preparation at all."

Your marketing content should follow the same rule. Take time to communicate with precision. Less is more in today's noisy world. Shorter content more frequently is more effective than longer content sent sporadically. In writing this book, I will probably delete as many words as I write. The editing process is challenging, time-consuming, and emotionally draining. But here's one thing I know: If you require your audience to sift through tons of rocks to find your nugget of gold, they will pass.

Patience

I love the 1 percent rule. It says small gains over time can create exponential results, like compound interest. The same principle applies to your marketing. As we have discussed, marketing is the precursor to sales. You will be frustrated if you try to attach a sales harvest to every marketing seed planted. The results are not always immediate, and the harvest takes time.

Water boils at 212 degrees. That's when things happen. In the right system, the steam generated at 212 degrees creates power that can operate many large machines. But when you put the water on the stove's burner, it doesn't convert to steam immediately. Instead, the temperature increases degree by degree until it finally hits 212. Often, we want our marketing to start at 211 so we only have one degree to go. That might work with a transactional marketing strategy, but building relationships takes time, especially when managing someone's money. Chemistry, trust, and integrity are earned over time. I've seen too many good marketing plans fail because of impatience. Don't take your marketing plan off the stove before it has a chance to reach 212.

Authenticity

Before the COVID-19 outbreak, most of the marketing content our company created for clients was in written form. Since COVID-19, a majority of the content is video. The advantage of video is that it allows your audience to read your words and see and hear them through your unique personality.

You don't have to be a TV news anchor to deliver great content via video. Just be yourself. One of the greatest compliments you can receive is for your audience to watch your video and feel like they are sitting in the same room with you.

The key is authenticity. The last thing you want is your marketing content to not represent who you are. Your clients are ultimately doing business with you, not just the service you provide.

When we started producing videos for our clients during COVID, their clients often responded, "It was great to see and hear from you." With today's news media, you often must use emotional energy to filter the content. As a financial advisor, you are a trusted voice for your clients. Therefore, your clients can sit back and consume your content without the emotional hoops to jump through. They trust who you are as long as they feel that you are being authentic. You don't need to create a different on-camera personality. Also, a prospect doesn't want to waste time getting to know you by video only to find out you are radically different when they meet you in person.

Sell Without Selling

I played tennis in college and spent three years as a tennis pro at a local country club after graduation.

One of my responsibilities was to stock our pro shop. I leased out the clothing portion because I knew that was an inventory nightmare, and I focused on the basics: shoes, rackets, and tennis balls.

One of my most successful marketing tools was purchasing a demo racket for each model I offered for sale. Time and again, a member would walk into the shop and pick up one of the new rackets. I would offer the demo as a "try before you buy," and they would always say, "I'm not looking for a new racket."

I responded, "That's OK. You don't need to buy it. You can try it—no pressure."

And almost 90 percent of the time, they would return and say, "OK. How much does it cost? I'll buy it."

I loved that because I was able to sell without selling. To me, that's the heart of marketing.

So how can you do the same? Be willing to give first and sell second. So what do I mean?

Offer things to both your clients and prospects with no strings attached. Be willing to nurture your client and prospect relationships unconditionally. Don't hesitate to offer free content, helpful tips, downloads, etc.

For prospects, it provides an opportunity to get to know you better. For clients, it reminds them of why they do business with you and the value you provide beyond their portfolio.

Communicate in Layers

There are lots of reasons you might listen to a great song. It could be the melody, great words, or your preferred tempo. But here's one thing I know: I doubt you would keep listening if the song contained only one note.

When you watch a great movie, I doubt you would stay engaged if the scene never changed and the actors repeated the same lines. Some movies fail because of a mundane plot that doesn't take the audience on an exciting journey.

When you listen to a great speech, I doubt the speaker speaks with the same speed and tone throughout the speech. Great speakers change their tone and cadence to keep you engaged.

An effective marketing plan is not one-dimensional. It needs to have layers. Therefore, don't communicate with just written content, just video, just print, just digital, just social media—you get my point. If your audience sees the same thing delivered in the same way over and over, they will soon turn the channel or walk out of your movie.

CONCLUSION

I was frustrated when we arrived at a client's office only to find they had not prepared for the day's video shoot. I loved the client, but my frustration stemmed from wanting to create the best content possible, and I felt we might not reach our goal for the day. My son, Fletcher, who works with me, could sense my frustration. I then noticed a text on my phone from Fletcher, even though he was standing three feet from me. It simply read, "Remember, incredibly kind." When he reminded me of one of our key values, my attitude quickly changed!

Embracing core marketing values will keep you focused on the mission at hand. Our values remind us *why* we do what we do. Too often, we launch into the how and what without considering the why. For every piece of marketing content you produce, make sure it passes your "values" test. If it doesn't, perhaps a valuable member of your team will text you a reminder!

PART 2

For your marketing strategy to produce fruit that will lead to a harvest, you have to prepare the soil for planting. Every financial advisor I meet is different. Although you might do similar things, the personality and DNA of your office are unique to you. In this section, let's talk about *you* and how to align *your* marketing strategy with *your* personality.

CHAPTER 6

WHAT'S YOUR MARKETING PERSONALITY?

It was the day for our leadership team to come together for our annual retreat. During this phase of my life, I owned a textile company, and I hired a consultant to help us understand how to work better as a team.

The first step was to take a personality test. At the time, Myers–Briggs was the most popular option available. Unfortunately, I can't remember the letters assigned to me when the results were complete, but I remember this.

One member of our leadership team was often misunderstood. He came across as arrogant, demanding, and insensitive at times. However, when his test results were announced, one member said, "Wow, you're not a jerk after all. I now see why you communicate the way you do."

So what's my point?

Although you have probably taken a personality inventory such as DISC, StrengthsFinder, or Myers-Briggs, do you know your "marketing" personality? In my work with financial advisors and their teams, I've found that almost everyone falls into one of these four categories:

- Adventurous Marketer
- Inspiring Marketer
- Dependable Marketer
- Deliberate Marketer

Why does this matter? You may frustrate your team if they don't understand which category you fall into. They may also frustrate you if you don't understand their marketing personality. Finally, you might frustrate yourself if your marketing plan is "deliberate" but your marketing personality is "adventurous."

I've always encouraged advisors to find a sustainable strategy. Too often, we start and stop because we run out of gas, or our strategy doesn't align with our personality, and we lose interest.

Want to know your marketing personality and the potential blind spots to be aware of? You can find out by taking a brief quiz at DiscoverBlindSpots.com/quiz.

But remember, it's also not advantageous to be one-dimensional. Although your personality inventory might identify a dominant trait, the combination of all the ingredients makes you unique. Your marketing content will favor your marketing personality, but you might need to stretch a little.

For example, I know several deliberate marketers. I love their attention to detail, but too often, they are tempted to stay in the weeds of perfection and never release any content. Remember, version one is always better than version zero. Perhaps a bit of adventurous marketing might help.

I also know several adventurous marketers. The blind spot for this personality is that you often get bored and want to try new things constantly, never sticking with a strategy. This will frustrate your team and your audience as they try to follow your message.

An ideal strategy includes a bit of all these strategies to speak to the variety of personalities you serve. Yes, it is *your* message, but you need to make sure it is a message that provides value to your audience. For example, I love writing with nice fountain pens, but if this book focused solely on how a fountain pen is better than a ballpoint, I doubt you would still be reading.

CONCLUSION

Your core message will flow more authentically if it represents who you are. It's also a lot easier! Advisors are sometimes tempted to follow someone else's plan, causing frustration with marginal results.

Whether you take this marketing personality inventory (DiscoverBlindSpots.com/quiz) or another personality inventory, at least take time to determine your core message. What's the one thing that makes you different from every other advisor? What are you passionate about that is easy to share with your clients and prospects? That passion should drive *your* marketing strategy.

CHAPTER 7

DEFINING YOUR 10 PERCENT

Recently, I talked to one of our clients and asked about his success. He lives in a town of two thousand people and is currently a solo advisor with two members of additional support staff. However, he has $200 million in assets under management. Now do I have your attention?

He said, "Tim, 90 percent of what I do, every other advisor does practically the same thing. So I focus on the 10 percent that makes us different."

So, what's the 10 percent for this advisor?

It's the older client I met in his office recently who mentioned that he just bought a new car but didn't know how to use all the fancy buttons and technology. So he asked this advisor if he could walk outside and take a look. However, this advisor is not a car expert—but his client thinks he is.

It's the couple who mentioned they are considering a dream vacation and asked for his recommendation. You got it—he's not a travel agent, but his clients still think he can help.

It's the client who finished a conversation at the conference table, and before he left, he said, "Oh, I can't leave yet; I need to walk around the corner." I was informed that this was a significant tradition after every client meeting. Each client walks around the corner of the conference room to the front office area. At that point, the two other staff members immediately stop what they are doing and love on the client for the next few minutes. It doesn't matter what is on their plate; they stop and give 100 percent of their attention to the client.

When the client walks out, they leave smiling and laughing. Those few minutes are more valuable to his clients than any discussion about their portfolios.

And finally, it's the marketing content that this advisor sends weekly to his clients that is not salesy but communicates that they care. In fact, one recent video was entitled, "Just Because We Love You."

What's the 10 percent that makes you and your office different? Too many times, I hear, "I'm just a financial advisor." Unfortunately, that's not good enough, and here's why.

Believe it or not, many people need help understanding what you do. For example, I know that a CPA does my taxes. I know that my doctor provides medical advice and care. I know that my lawyer handles my legal needs. I know my pastor provides spiritual insight. But as a financial advisor, you often wear parts of all these hats with your clients.

Elevator Pitch

What's your elevator pitch? What do you say when you get that dreaded question about what you do?

You are out at a cocktail party or event. Someone walks up and introduces themselves. After the pleasantries, the same question always comes up: "So, what do you do?"

Your go-to response is, "I'm a financial advisor" or "I work for a financial advisory firm." Or you might ramble on describing the "things" you do, and with every sentence, it becomes less and less clear. Typically, that leads the person to move on to the next topic, or that's their cue to exit the conversation.

But what if your answer caused someone to say, "Wow, tell me more."

You might call it your elevator pitch; every person in your firm needs one, and it helps if they are the same.

What's a great elevator pitch? It usually has three parts.

- State the problem.
- State the solution.
- State the transformation that can take place when the problem is solved.

Here's an example for a financial advisor: "Managing your finances in today's world can be confusing. There are many options, and choosing the right strategy can feel overwhelming. We simplify the process, so you don't have to live your life wondering whether you are making the right financial decisions."

Now, isn't that better than saying "I'm a financial advisor" or "I work for a financial advisory firm"?

And finally, your marketing should incorporate your elevator pitch through your website, social media, and emails. Defining your 10 percent and finding the words to communicate it will cause your audience to want to know more.

My advisor client at the beginning of this Chapter would say: "Money can be complicated at times. We bring clarity to our clients' financial decisions while loving them where they are and walking with them throughout their entire financial journey to reach their preferred destination."

CONCLUSION

When interviewing a financial advisor client for a video shoot, I often ask, "What makes you different?" In essence, I want to know their 10 percent. Some have an immediate answer, but others have to think for a minute. It's not that they don't have something that makes them unique; usually, they minimize it or take it for granted. In my years of working with financial advisor firms, I've never met two that were the same. Each office has its own DNA and unique qualities.

Take a few minutes and make a list of your 10 percent. Ask your staff to do the same and compare notes. Next, see if you can put it into an elevator pitch that you can use the next time you get asked, "So, what do you do?"

CHAPTER 8

DEFINING YOUR AUDIENCE

When our company, Discover Blind Spots, works with a new financial advisor, I always ask for a two-hour kickoff session with the team. The session focuses on the culture of the advisors' practice. One of the questions we ask is about identifying the ideal client.

I remember several years ago asking this question, and to this date, it ranks as one of my favorite answers. The founding partner said, "Our ideal client is someone who wants to do business with us as much as we want to do business with them." He said, "Tim, I've been doing this a long time. I know all the tricks to convince someone to become a client. But I have learned over the years that it never works in the long term when I force that relationship." I love the wisdom in this comment.

Too many times, marketing content doesn't consider the audience it is intended for. Before I speak to a group, the first question I ask the host is who will be attending. I may have a great message, but it is meaningless to the wrong audience. Although you might feel that your audience is a compilation of all types, dig a little.

To narrow your focus, ask these questions: What is the average age of your clients? What are their vocations? Are they pre-retirement, close to retirement, or post-retirement? What specific problems does each of these groups face? The more you are clear about your audience, the more effective your message will be.

But, for the sake of time in this Chapter, let's simplify. You basically have two audiences: clients and prospects. And you need to determine the amount of time and energy you will devote your marketing content for each group.

Some advisors we work with focus 100 percent of their effort on clients. They've worked hard to build their business and don't have the capacity or energy to add new clients at this stage in their careers. Others are in growth mode and trying to implement a strategy to speak to prospects. Still others spend time on both.

A healthy strategy starts with clients and then moves to prospects. Why?

Clients

Clients are a warm audience that you want to avoid getting cold. Remember, 65 percent of clients who leave do so because of indifference. Clients must be reminded of why they do business with you—especially in a down market, when their portfolios create doubt.

I love the story of one advisor we work with who shared an email he received from his top client. Typically when we start working with an advisor, we shoot an interview with each team member. The goal is to share the heart behind why they do what they do. It's a great way to remind your clients how much you care.

After sending this advisor's video, he received an email response from one of his top clients a few hours later. He shared with me the tension he felt regarding how often to communicate with this client. He wanted to be proactive and responsive but did not want to be a nuisance. The email he received back read, "Thanks for taking the time to send this. My wife and I both watched your video, and it reminded us of why we do business with you." That video and response was invaluable to this advisor.

Remember, your clients need reminders of who you are and why you do what you do.

I once heard a leader discuss how often you should share your vision with your audience. He said, "You cast vision over and over and over. And when finished, you cast it over and over and over again." And as we discussed in Chapter 4, the clearer your message to your clients, the more likely they will talk about you, which leads me to my next point.

Referrals are a vital part of a financial advisor's success. But the old way of asking for referrals is not effective anymore. Guilting clients into providing their friends' and relatives' names is awkward. No client wants to do this. However, if the vision of what you do, who you are, and the problems you solve are clear to your clients, they will talk about you without being asked.

Here's a subtle paradigm shift for referrals. Use your marketing content for your clients to talk about problems you can solve. Your client may not have that problem, but chances are they know somebody who does. When that happens, your client is motivated to offer *you* as a solution to help their friend or family member. So move the spotlight from you to your client. Let them be the hero of the story with their friends and family.

Prospects

Once you have a consistent and sustainable strategy for clients, let's move to prospects. The old way of prospecting is to "get a name" and make a connection. If they say yes, great. If they are not ready, you set a reminder to call them in three months to follow up. Soon you start to feel like a stalker!

What if you change the strategy, remove your sales hat, and provide value to the prospect first, all before the sale? When you make a connection, and they are not ready, slowly send content that addresses potential problems they might struggle with. Stay top of mind so you will be the first person they call when a life event happens.

I know an advisor who closed a prospect who had been on his list for eight years. He would try to remember to call at various times to check in, but it always felt like a sales call that nobody wanted to answer. But, eventually, this prospect had a life event that required a financial decision. Because this advisor had started sending helpful "non-salesy" content to this prospect, he was the first person the prospect called. His unconditional content allowed him to bridge the gap in the relationship.

CONCLUSION

Nothing is more powerful than someone willing to provide unconditional value in your life. It's the most compelling way to sell without selling. Yes, you need to be profitable, but the last thing you want to do is appear desperate to a prospect or a client. Asking for the sale too soon can send the wrong message about how you value relationships. We all know people who call only when they want something. Don't be that person!

Knowing your audience and refining your message to speak specifically to each group is vital. It will help you keep clients and close prospects who want to do business with you as much as you want to do business with them.

CHAPTER 9

DEFINING YOUR RHYTHM

During a kickoff session, I was sitting in a conference room with a financial advisor team. It was early in my marketing career, and I was excited to share everything we could do. But, unfortunately, I admit I fell into the trap of thinking that the more we could offer, the more valuable we would appear to our client.

Although they initially seemed excited, I could see their eyes glaze over with marketing overload. The excitement of implementing a new marketing plan was overshadowed by the fear of the time and energy it would take. After all, this team needed to focus on client meetings and portfolio management. They didn't have empty blocks of time to devote to marketing.

That's when the lead advisor of the practice said, "Tim, we are excited, but I would like to start with sending one piece of content each month." That's when I realized that setting the expectations early for the rhythm you can sustain is critical for the long-term success of your marketing plan. It's been a few years, and this client still sends one piece of content each month. Usually, it's a 2-3-minute video update for his clients. He realized the strategy's effectiveness when he had to miss a month and clients inquired because they valued the update each month. Because of his consistent rhythm, his marketing strategy has been successful and sustainable.

Sustainability

Before you launch into a discussion about all the things you can do, determine a sustainable rhythm. Random marketing is the quickest way to lose your audience. Remember, effective marketing is about excellent communication to build and nurture relationships. We've all had people randomly show up in our lives and then disappear. Usually, they show up when they need something and disappear when they don't. The quickest way to lose your audience is to show up only when you want something.

Although *you* have to determine the right rhythm you and your team can sustain, here are a few guidelines to consider.

First, I recommend communicating at least once per month. Any less, and you may have to spend time reminding your audience why you are communicating. Less than once a month feels sporadic, and you lose continuity from one message to another. You want your messages to build upon each other, not start from scratch each time.

However, I also recommend to clients that once per week is not too much. Sometimes when I make this recommendation, a client will respond, "But our clients will unsubscribe if we send content each week!" That's when I ask about the type of content sent in the past. Typically it's canned content that does not represent their voice to their audience. If you take the time to share your voice, thoughts, wisdom, and knowledge, your audience will welcome the communication. Your rhythm should correlate with your ability to sustain, not your audience's ability to consume.

I am often asked about the perfect length for a video or written content. Your content should be as long as it is still engaging. If it loses effectiveness after one paragraph or thirty seconds, that's how long it should be. On the contrary, you might be OK if it stays relevant and engaging for five pages or ten minutes. However, usually, shorter content with a consistent rhythm is best for you and your audience.

Rhythm Requires Focus

The longer I live, the more I've come to realize that one characteristic separates great leaders from average leaders: focus.

If you're like me, my most productive days are when I stay laser-focused on the most critical projects that will make a difference in moving my company forward.

But sometimes it's hard. I have great intentions, but stuff gets in the way. Sometimes I love doing the little things. It feels good to check off many small to-dos from my daily list.

But at the end of the day, did it make a difference?

The same is true for your marketing strategy. Because marketing is planting seeds that you hope will eventually produce a harvest, it's easy to put it off until tomorrow or the next day, next week, or next year.

And since we are an instant gratification culture, why spend time on something today that doesn't produce immediate results?

The best marketers identify a clear plan and stick with it. Sure, they make adjustments along the way, but focusing on a sustainable rhythm is essential to the strategy.

CONCLUSION

I had a life goal of running a marathon several years ago. I trained, and I was ready. But as the race began, I allowed my excitement to get the best of me. I ran the first 13 miles at a record pace but developed cramps and almost could not finish the race. I crossed the finish line in pretty bad shape.

Marketing is a marathon, not a sprint. I remember passing many people in the race's first half only to see them pass by me in the second half. Your audience wants to know that you will be there for the entirety of the race. Make sure your marketing rhythm provides the assurance they need.

CHAPTER 10

WHO WILL COMMUNICATE TO WHOM?

On a podcast I listened to recently, a marketing guru was talking about a few marketing challenges that get in the way. I would call them blind spots. One was to determine how your content will be delivered before you create the content. Too often, we waste time creating marketing content without thinking about how it will be distributed and to whom.

Several years ago, a prospect asked our company to shoot a series of videos. They said, "We don't need all the other services, just videos." I then asked whether they planned to distribute the videos by email, website, or social media, and about the intended audience. I noticed the silence on the other end of the call. Next, I asked about their plans for creating landing pages with clear calls to action. I finally asked whether they planned to use YouTube, Vimeo, or another site to store the videos. They said, "I don't know…I guess we have a few decisions to make." My point was not to create frustration but to eliminate potential headaches in the future. The answers to those questions are not complicated, but when overlooked, they cause great content to sit on the shelf without a plan of action.

Solo or Team?

If you are a solo advisor, your message should come from you to both your clients and prospects. However, if you have a staff member who usually helps on-ramp new clients, their voice may be helpful for this type of content.

If you are an office with multiple advisors, do you usually communicate as a team, or does each advisor work solely with their clients? If you are a team, allow the team to communicate. However, make sure that each team member's message is clear and consistent. A content series with a consistent theme is a great way to provide continuity with multiple voices.

If your team works specifically with their clients and prospects, ensure each voice can communicate with its audience. The purpose of your content is to develop and nurture those relationships, so a consistent voice is helpful.

Credibility

As a communicator, you should have credibility with your audience. The best way to leverage that credibility is to communicate to an audience that knows you or is clear on your role within the organization. Confusion will often follow if you are not clear about who is communicating and why they are communicating to a particular audience.

My wife, Stacy, expects me to communicate directly with her in our marriage. Asking one of my children or a friend to speak on my behalf is not a good plan if I want to keep that relationship. I love the idea of multiple voices, but those voices are more powerful if they have credibility with their audience.

One final note: Don't ask someone to communicate who doesn't have the authority or credibility to respond to questions or comments from your audience. Many years ago, I had a personal banker who handled my account. Although I had a relationship with him and we met often, I quickly realized he didn't have authority to make decisions. The decision maker was never visible and preferred to remain hidden in an office. Soon, my personal banker's voice lost its effectiveness and credibility.

Recently, an event planner contacted me for a speaking engagement. When I asked about the audience, she said it was a group of symphony leaders throughout the southeast. Now, I love music, but I quickly passed because I don't have credibility with this group.

So don't skip over what might appear obvious. The quality of your content is important, but who communicates that content to whom is just as important.

CONCLUSION

One final thing to remember: If you are launching a new marketing campaign to clients, explain why they are receiving the content. For example, if you want to send a video series about retirement to your clients, lead with an email stating that you value communication and that over the next several weeks, you want to share some helpful tips. If the entire team plans to communicate, tell your clients that each team member will provide their thoughts and ideas.

For prospects, I thank them for opting in to receive the content and briefly tell them what to expect in the coming weeks or months. I even invite them to unsubscribe if they don't feel that the content is helpful.

Always lay out the plan for your audience. Don't leave your audience asking why. Clarity is key! We've all received an email and asked, "Who is this, and why are they sending it to me?" Unfortunately, confusion often leads to the delete button.

CHAPTER 11

CONTENT: WHERE DO I START?

Have you ever had writer's block? Or in today's world, maybe creative content block? It's funny how sometimes things flow, and other times, well, not so much. But that blank canvas waiting for your next big idea can feel overwhelming.

How do you stay out of ruts and ensure your marketing communication to clients and prospects doesn't start to feel one-dimensional?

Here's a tip. Your marketing content should align with your personality. (Remember to take the quick survey in Chapter 6 to determine your marketing personality.) Most content falls into one of these three categories.

1. Education
2. Entertainment
3. Inspiration

If you love to teach, your content will be more educational. If you love the camera, your content might be more entertaining. If you are highly relational, you might focus on inspiration. I suspect that you will create from who you are, and a majority of your content will fall into one of those three categories. If you are struggling with content block, start with the category that aligns with your personality.

But the best content strategy includes a little of all three.

Mix It Up

Like I always say, you should communicate in layers, so mix it up. Remember, people consume in layers too. Eating the same food day after day can get boring. Don't feed them grilled chicken all the time. Instead, mix in a pizza, steak, or even a scoop of ice cream every now and then. You might be surprised by the results!

One of our clients, who usually communicates from the educational category, created a video about "National Napping Day." He briefly informed his audience that this particular day, the Monday after "spring forward," was dedicated to taking a nap. He encouraged everyone to celebrate this national holiday. At the end of the video, he challenged his audience to find time to recoup that lost hour of sleep as he raised his pillow and walked off camera. His audience loved it because it showed a different side of his personality.

Remember, your content can focus on something other than financial topics. As you will recall in Chapter 7, a financial advisor wears many hats. Sometimes you play the role of a counselor, friend, and mentor, so your content should represent all these roles.

More Than a Financial Advisor

Here's something to consider. How can you use your marketing content to broaden the perspective of how your audience sees you? How can you move from being a trusted financial advisor to a trusted advisor?

Most financial advisors have clients who view their relationship beyond financial topics. Usually, those clients become lifelong relationships. Why? Because your relationship has moved beyond the numbers on a spreadsheet. Your clients may have initially contacted you because of your expertise, but they move to lifelong clients when they learn who you are below the neck. Sharing those different parts of your personality is vital to growing your relationships.

When my wife Stacy and I started dating, she knew me only as a fellow college student. When we got married, I became a husband. When we had children, I added the role of parent. When my oldest daughter, Ragan, was diagnosed with cancer during her senior year of college, Stacy saw me as a caregiver. (Ragan is cancer-free today, by the way!) When I started my business, Stacy saw the entrepreneur part of my personality. We now have grandkids, which has uncovered a whole new name for me: Poppy. All of these experiences enhanced and grew our relationship over the years.

Client relationships follow a similar path. The problem is time. You don't have enough hours to share the different sides of your personality with your clients or prospects face-to-face. You might chit-chat before a portfolio review, but building relationships takes time. In today's digital world, your marketing communication can help share the many facets of who you are.

CONCLUSION

If you feel overwhelmed trying to determine what your marketing content should look like, start in the most comfortable category for you, the one that aligns with your personality. Spend 70 percent of your time on education, entertainment, or inspiration. But stretch yourself with the other categories 30 percent of the time. Remember, you are not one-dimensional; as long as you are authentic, your audience will enjoy getting to know the real you!

PART 3

My hope for this book was to present not just theory but practicality. Over the past two sections, I have offered a different perspective on marketing, providing foundational principles that can support your strategy. Consider those sections the aerial view to allow you to see where you might go.

In this section, I want to provide practical steps you can apply on your own or through working with a marketing company. This next section includes helpful tips our clients have implemented to nurture relationships with their audiences over the past years, ultimately leading to a few harvests.

Enjoy!

CHAPTER 12
BEFORE YOU GET STARTED

Over the years of working with advisors on their marketing plans, the most significant obstacles are distractions. You have great intentions today, but what if markets go crazy tomorrow, diverting all your attention? What if you have grown your business to such a point that you don't feel you need to continue your marketing efforts? What if you get bored with your plan? What if you get impatient and wonder whether it will ever produce a harvest?

The Messy Middle
It's always great to start something, and it's great to finish it, but somewhere in the middle, we get distracted and lose sight of the purpose. When I work with leaders, helping them set goals, I encourage them to write a "why" statement for each goal. In essence, why is this goal important? Why does it deserve your attention? Then, when you reach the messy middle, read your "why" statement to remind you.

So, why don't you pause here and quickly write down a "why" statement for starting your new marketing plan or reviewing and adjusting your existing plan? As you write, remember these principles.

- Great marketing equals great communication.
- Great communication leads to great relationships.
- Marketing is not the same as sales.
- Marketing is the planting, and sales is the harvest.

Now that you know why, remember that marketing is a marathon, not a sprint. Don't sprint out of the box too fast and run out of gas. Don't let your vision be larger than your feet can take you. There are only twenty-four hours in a day, and I don't think that will change anytime soon! You have a business to run and a life outside your business. Don't allow your marketing plan to rule your life.

Start small, be consistent, evaluate, adjust, and add new ideas as needed. Be patient to allow your plan to produce some fruit, but don't expect perfection out of the gate. Instead, find your voice and what works best for you.

The following Chapters are not a one-size-fits-all plan. Some ideas might work for you, and others might not. But don't be afraid to step out of your comfort zone. Remember that your first written content, first video, and first printed flyer will never be your best. But version one is always better than version zero. Seek input from others, but don't fall victim to death by committee. Don't just focus on what people say but look beneath the words for the nuggets you can build on.

And finally, remember, your marketing plan is for your audience, not you. I know marketers who love to hear themselves talk. Your audience can smell this type of arrogance. Usually, your marketing content will come from two buckets. One is authority, and the other is empathy. The more empathy, the less authority you need. People don't care how much you know until they know how much you care. As a financial advisor, you are in a relationship business, not a transactional one. If your audience doesn't quickly see that your content provides value, they will get bored and turn the channel. Nurture relationships first until you earn the right to ask for the sale.

CONCLUSION

Recently, I had an advisor look at a website we had completed for a new client. They said, "I want the same thing; just duplicate what they have." I reminded them that their voice was unique and we needed to focus on sharing it.

Remember, a marketing plan is not something you purchase and implement. The most successful plans are unique to you, your voice, your personality, and your audience.

Action Steps

- Write down a few "why" statements for your marketing goals.

- Take the marketing personality quiz at www.DiscoverBlindSpots.com/quiz.

- Reflect on the categories your voice best represents for your audience:

  - educational, entertaining, or inspirational. Pick one and start a list of potential content you could create from this category.

CHAPTER 13

USING AUTOMATION

Creating content is one thing, but don't forget how it will be delivered. In the old days, most content was either printed and mailed or on TV as a commercial. In today's digital world, with email, social media, and websites, it is much easier to share content. But don't overlook the system you will use to deliver your content. Let's start with your most valuable deliverable method, email.

There are tons of systems available that you can use to deliver your marketing content. Unfortunately, as a financial advisor, you probably have limited options because of compliance restrictions and the need for a system to archive your communications.

Some systems are simple; they focus on the ease of delivering an email to a large group of contacts. Others provide more options, allowing you to automatically move to the next step when an action happens. For example, "seven days after this email, deliver the next email" or "if a contact doesn't click on a link, wait three days and send a reminder." Another benefit is creating a campaign with months of content set to be delivered to a specific group at a specific time without manually releasing them individually.

The system we use for most of our clients is Keap. It addresses the compliance requirements for most advisors and provides helpful automation to fit your needs. (More at Keap.com or contact me at DiscoverBlindSpots.com).

Once you find the right solution, here are a few tips as you begin implementation.

Good Automation Versus Bad Automation

Automation strategies are not created equal. There are good practices and bad. For example, we've all received an email that screamed spam or canned as it was sitting in our inbox. Remember, using automation is not an excuse for being lazy. Good automation allows you to be more efficient, but you must pay attention to a few things to ensure it is effective.

One simple tip is to always send your email from a person, not info@yourfirmname. Sometimes an advisor will suggest that if they use their email, they will be overwhelmed with responses after a client or prospect receives their content. The response I want to use is, "You are not that important!" but I typically respond by asking, "Isn't that what you want? Don't you want your audience to engage with you?" Trust me, if your audience replies to your marketing content, you will love it. There is no better feeling than seeing those replies in your inbox.

Next, try to use a salutation, and make sure you are sending to a familiar name. For example, my full name is Timothy, but everyone calls me Tim. When I receive an email to Dear Timothy, I quickly know that the sender doesn't really know me. When my parents called me by my full name, I knew it was important, but marketing emails, not so much. Therefore, prepare your contacts with the correct familiar name before entering them into your marketing system.

Narrow Your Audience

At first, your marketing message will usually have a broad audience. Initially, you will probably default to sending to all your contacts. However, if you think you can speak to everyone, you might find that you can speak to no one. What do I mean?

Eventually, you will want to narrow your audience and speak to specific groups. For example, you may categorize your clients as A, B, or C. Your message to an A client might differ from that to a C client. You may create content that speaks to widows, couples, business owners, pre-retirement, post-retirement–you get my point. The more your content is focused on a specific audience, the better. A sound marketing system will allow you to do this with ease.

Access to Data

Finally, one of the biggest reasons to use a marketing system to deliver your content is to gain access to data. If you send content from your regular email system, you probably don't have access to whether the contact opens the email, clicks on a video link, or downloads a document. Remember, your marketing content is not for you, it's for your audience. If they don't engage, you are wasting your time.

Without engagement data, you are operating blind. Wouldn't knowing which contacts are opening each email and either reading or watching your content be helpful? On the flip side, perhaps even more valuable is to know those who aren't. Think about prospects. How valuable would it be to know whether a prospect has been engaging with your content before you contact them with a follow-up call? If you have been sending content for six months and they haven't opened one email, chances are they won't know you when you call—or even answer the phone.

Finally, access to this type of data helps eliminate the vocal minority. For example, I know an advisor who thought his audience loved his technical content. When I asked how, he said he always receives feedback from a client praising his content. When we looked at the numbers, he realized that only 5 percent of his audience opened the emails and watched his technical videos. Without this data, he might be misled into thinking that one client represents the needs of his entire audience.

CONCLUSION

Most of your time will be spent creating the right content for your audience, but don't forget the importance of delivering the content with the right kind of automation to manage the workload. You don't need a marketing system to start, but it is something to consider as your strategy grows. Eventually, you will want to do more, so automating the process is critical for sustainability.

Action Steps

- Research marketing systems that are available for you to use.

- Write down automation capabilities that will be helpful to you and check them off your list as you evaluate these systems.

- Identify who will manage the system daily. The more you work with a new system, the more efficient you will be. Of course, it's great for your entire team to have access, but I have found that assigning one person to manage is best.

CHAPTER 14

EMAIL IS NOT DEAD

In an era in which social media platforms and chatbots dominate the digital marketing landscape, one might assume that email marketing has lost its effectiveness. However, despite the rise of various marketing technologies, email remains the undisputed king of marketing tools. According to Statista, the global number of email users is expected to grow to 4.6 billion by 2025. With such a vast user base, it's no wonder that email continues to reign supreme in the marketing world. Also, in 2020, the global email marketing market was valued at $7.5 billion and is projected to increase to $17.9 billion by 2027—not a bad growth projection! Here are a few reasons why.

Universal Access and Compatibility

One of the main reasons email remains an unrivaled marketing tool is its widespread accessibility and compatibility. With billions of users worldwide, email transcends generational, geographical, and cultural boundaries. Unlike social media platforms that cater to specific demographics and require frequent updates, email is available to everyone with an internet connection. In addition, it can be accessed on a wide range of devices, from desktop computers to smartphones.

Personalization and Segmentation

Email marketing allows you to segment your audience based on various factors, such as demographics, preferences, and behaviors. This level of segmentation enables you to send highly personalized messages to your contacts, improving engagement and conversion rates. With the help of advanced email marketing platforms, you can automate your campaigns to ensure that each contact receives the most relevant content at the right time.

Easy to Track and Measure

Another advantage of email marketing is that it is easy to track and measure the success of your campaigns. Most email marketing platforms provide detailed analytics on open rates, click-through rates, conversions, and more. This enables you to evaluate the effectiveness of your campaigns and make data-driven decisions to improve your marketing strategies.

Builds Trust and Relationships

Email marketing lets you consistently stay in touch with your customers and prospects. You can build trust and establish a long-term relationship with your audience by providing valuable content. This ongoing engagement can increase client loyalty and positive word-of-mouth referrals.

High Engagement Rates
Great marketing content is only valuable if your audience engages. Let's compare engagement between email and social media. How many social media posts do you view daily compared with the total you have available? Even though you may think that you scroll for hours each day, the percentage is still low compared with what's available.

Now compare that with email. What percentage of emails do you receive that you at least look at the sender and read the subject line? The number is probably high. Most don't delete emails without scanning through them to determine what to ignore and what to engage. There is tremendous value in your name and subject line being visible to your contacts consistently.

Don't Get Lazy
Even with all the above data, I am not naive in thinking that your contacts will always read your emails. Email open rates have declined over the years, but that's not because the technology has lost relevance. Unfortunately, we have gotten lazy with email creation, causing our audience to sift through the junk to find value. But here's how to dramatically increase your engagement with your audience.

Provide Wisdom Along with Knowledge

Emails have become challenging because most emails we receive deliver information instead of wisdom. The mind can hold only so much information before it checks out, but it will make space for wisdom. Most advisors default to communicating knowledge, which is OK, but make sure your knowledge includes a few wisdom nuggets along the way. Don't just focus on what; include the how and why. Emails that leave you asking how and why lose effectiveness over time.

Keep It Simple: One Topic at a Time

Although you might be tempted to think you are working smarter, not harder, by including multiple topics in an email, don't do it. Yes, it's nice to know you can put all your thoughts in one email, but your audience will not see it that way. Stay on point with your topic. Resist the urge to include everything you are thinking. If you have multiple topics you want to communicate about retirement, for example, create a series of emails with one topic per email. Here's a great reminder from Tom Stoppard: "Good things, when short, are twice as good."

Use Short Words, Short Sentences, and Short Paragraphs

Remember, beware of the curse of knowledge explained in Chapter 4. Refrain from requiring your audience to research obscure words you use. You might think this tip results from today's digital world filled with short cryptic messages, but it has been around for a bit.

"Use familiar words—words that your readers will understand, and not words they will have to look up. No advice is more elementary, and no advice is more difficult to accept. When we feel an impulse to use a marvelously exotic word, let us lie down until the impulse goes away." –James J. Kilpatrick (1920-2010)

Make Sure You Have Lots of White Space

If you follow the previous tip of short words, sentences, and paragraphs, you will have lots of white space. White space refers to space around your content and within it. Nobody wants to get an email with a giant blob of text. It is not appealing to see or read. Because more and more emails are read on phones and tablets, the last thing your audience wants to do is scroll forever to reach the next paragraph. I often keep paragraphs to three sentences max, and most paragraphs are one or two sentences long.

Do This	Don't Do This
This is an example of lots of white space. This is an example of lots of white space. This is an example of lots of white space. This is an example of lots of white space. This is an example of lots of white space. This is an example of lots of white space. This is an example of lots of white space. This is an example of lots of white space. This is an example of lots of white space.	This is **NOT** an example of lots of white space. This is **NOT** an example of lots of white space. This is **NOT** an example of lots of white space. This is **NOT** an example of lots of white space. This is **NOT** an example of lots of white space. This is **NOT** an example of lots of white space. This is **NOT** an example of lots of white space. This is **NOT** an example of lots of white space. This is **NOT** an example of lots of white space. This is **NOT** an example of lots of white space. This is **NOT** an example of lots of white space. This is **NOT** an example of lots of white space.

Bullets and Lists Are Helpful

When you have multiple points you are making about a single topic, convert them to bullets or a numbered list. A list helps your audience organize the content to make it memorable. In addition, you demonstrate kindness to your audience when you provide bullets and lists. It's as if you say, "I have done tons of research, and I am going to save you time by sharing the most important points." Don't make your audience create their own outline to remember your content.

Make It Personal, Not Corporate

As I mentioned in Chapter 13, emails should be sent from a person to a person. So when I receive an email asking me to respond, and I hit reply and notice the email address is info@companyname, I delete it and move on. Remember, people don't create relationships with companies; they create relationships with people. And don't worry about too many replies flooding your inbox. But if it happens, that's a good problem to have.

Don't Forget the Importance of the Subject Line

Your subject line is the door to your email. Refrain from writing lazy subject lines that tell your audience what's in the email. Don't allow them to assume they know what you are saying before you say it. Questions are great subject lines because they require your audience to open the email to find the answer. For example: Do You Know the Perfect Time to Take Social Security?

Also, half sentences work well, followed by an ellipsis. For example, "I noticed a funny look on my client's face and…" When I see this in a subject line, I want to open the email to find the rest of the sentence.

Have One Clear Call to Action

Don't leave your audience wondering what to do after they consume your content. Not every piece of content requires a call to action, but if it does, make it clear. Buttons or links that say "click here" are helpful. Be clear about what you want your audience to do after consuming your content. However, don't turn your email into a billboard with multiple requests. If you do, your audience will feel like they are on a treasure hunt trying to find the next step. Keep it focused and simple.

CONCLUSION

While new marketing technologies and platforms will continue to emerge, email remains the most effective and reliable marketing tool available today and will likely continue to be so. Remember that email is a platform you own where you can send your content to whoever you want, when you want, and how you want. On other platforms, you must abide by a list of rules that are constantly changing.

Action Steps

Create a checklist with these eight questions to ask each time you complete your content:

1. Did I provide enough wisdom in addition to my knowledge?

2. Did I keep it simple, only focusing on one topic?

3. Did I use short words, sentences, and paragraphs?

4. Do I have lots of white space?

5. Do I need to create a few bullets or a list to help my audience remember the content?

6. Am I sending the content from my email address, not info@companyname?

7. Do I have an engaging subject line that causes the reader to want to know more?

8. Do I have a clear call to action?

CHAPTER 15

HOW TO USE VIDEO

Recent studies show that 86 percent of businesses use video for their marketing content and that 94 percent will continue to do so. Communication by video is not losing steam anytime soon. In the past five years, our creation of video content for our financial advisor clients has increased from 30 percent to 80 percent.

In today's fast-paced digital landscape, businesses continually seek innovative strategies to captivate their target audiences and foster brand loyalty. As a result, video content has emerged as a powerful medium to deliver remarkable results consistently.

Here's *why* you should find a way to use video, and later in the Chapter, I will discuss *how* you can begin to use it.

WHY USE VIDEO

Improved Engagement
Video content is more visually appealing to capture viewers' attention and keep them engaged for longer. Your audience will consume content in three primary ways: reading, listening, and watching. Research shows that engagement increases when you combine all of those means of consumption in video.

Emotional Connection
Video allows businesses to connect emotionally with their audience through storytelling, visuals, and audio elements. This emotional connection can help build trust, loyalty, and a stronger relationship between you and your audience.

For example, we recently had a financial advisor who wanted to connect with a potential prospect for years but had yet to succeed. The prospect was a daughter of a current client. No matter how often the mother talked about how much she valued the advisor, the daughter ignored her comments. Finally, when the advisor started using video, the mother forwarded one of the videos to her daughter. Immediately, the daughter set an appointment because she felt a connection with the advisor.

Easy to Consume and Share
Videos are easily consumable and shareable. As mentioned above, what better way for a client to share who you are with

their friends and family? Video is easily shareable on various social media platforms, helping viewers get to know your personality. We often hear advisors say that prospects feel they already know the advisor before their first meeting.

Recently, one of our advisor clients shared that they closed two new clients in recent months because an existing client was sharing their videos. During the initial meeting, the new client said, "I feel like I already know you from watching all your videos."

Video can help bridge those relational roadblocks. Video can also deepen your relationships with clients, allowing them to feel connected between face-to-face meetings.

Multi-Purpose

You can repurpose your video for various platforms so your content can have a broader reach. For example, after sending a video by email, you can upload it to social media and add it to your website. This versatility enables you to reach different audiences and achieve multiple marketing objectives with the same content. For example, quotes from a thought leadership video are great sound bites for social media.

HOW TO USE VIDEO

Now let's talk about how. I often hear advisors reference the complexity of video and the difficulty of devoting the time to produce content. But, also, how do you deliver it?

Let's start with the actual creation of the video content. There are two approaches: shoot it yourself or hire a company to shoot it for you.

Shooting Your Video Yourself

As we see on social media, our phones have become significant sources for producing video. If you use a phone, remember to shoot at a close range to fill the screen and capture decent audio if you don't have an external microphone. Audio is sometimes more critical than video. We consume all types of video quality, but your audience won't continue listening to bad audio.

Although shooting video yourself is cost-effective, it is often not time effective. I've heard horror stories of advisors spending hours trying to shoot video while assuming the role of creator, producer, videographer, and talent on camera. If you choose to shoot your own content, keep it simple. Don't spend all day trying to shoot a three-minute video.

Once your video is complete, you must decide where it will be consumed. I recommend emailing the video to your audience first, then posting it on social media and your website a few days later. Contacts who provide their email deserve to see the content first. A client is your innermost circle, followed by prospects and then your social media followers. Release your content in that order.

And finally, remember the thumbnails and written content that invite someone to watch your video. The copy that sets up a video is similar to the subject line for an email. Create a reason for your audience to watch. Don't assume they will click on your video solely because of your smiling face on the thumbnail.

Hiring Someone to Shoot Video for You

Although hiring someone to shoot video for you is an expense, the expertise and time efficiencies might be worth it. If you hire someone, you can focus on the content you deliver instead of all the other distractions.

There are two types of companies to consider. One is solely a video company. Typically you hire them for a day, and they will set up and shoot the number of videos you agree upon. The deliverable is usually a video file, and you still have to create thumbnails and landing pages and write copy based on the distribution of the video.

A second option is to hire a marketing company that offers video as a marketing solution. It's also helpful if you can find someone who understands your market to provide coaching with content. That is what we do at Discover Blind Spots.

This Chapter is not an advertisement for our services. Still, we work solely with financial advisors. We write video scripts, shoot, edit, add animations and graphics, create landing pages and thumbnails, and write copy to encourage your audience to watch your video. We can usually shoot twenty to forty videos in one day, depending on the content, which is incredibly time-efficient. After the shoot, you can return to running your business, and we take care of the rest.

I recommend this second option, whether it is working with our team or another company that provides a similar service. For example, consider a client who hires you to simplify their entire financial life instead of a few pieces. I'm sure you have found that to be a more effective strategy and use of time for your client.

CONCLUSION

No matter which direction you choose, get started. The video train to communicate your marketing message has left the station. It's not too late to get on board, but this train is picking up more steam every year. Start small and grow from there. You don't have to produce an Emmy-worthy performance; just be you. Share your personality with your audience!

Action Steps

- Map out the amount of video content you feel you can produce.

- Start with a series that provides continuity.

- Evaluate whether you have time to shoot it yourself or need to find a video or marketing company to shoot it for you.

- Pick a great thumbnail; your smiling face is a good start.

- Write copy to encourage your audience to watch your video.

- Decide where your audience can see your video (e.g., on a landing page, a website, YouTube, or Vimeo).

- Decide how to distribute your video (e.g., email, website, or social media).

CHAPTER 16

BECOMING A THOUGHT LEADER

Let's face it, one of the reasons you might resist implementing a marketing strategy is that the idea can feel salesy. Although you may have a well-established firm, cold calling and pitching your services might not top your list of things you love to do.

However, I bet you love sharing your knowledge, expertise, thoughts, and wisdom with your clients. How often have you finished conversing with a client, shared a nugget of wisdom, and wished all your clients were in the room? An easy way to solve this problem is to use your marketing to position yourself as a thought leader.

In the ever-evolving marketing world, standing out among the competition can be daunting. Embracing thought leadership as part of your marketing strategy offers an invaluable opportunity to differentiate yourself and establish trust and credibility with your audience. By sharing innovative ideas, insights, and solutions, you can elevate your brand, develop meaningful relationships, and provide an easy way for your audience to talk about you to others.

As a financial advisor, here is a starter list of topics to consider:

- Long-Term Care
- Identity Theft
- Social Security
- Starting Your Financial Plan
- Aging Parents
- Post-Separation Financial Challenges
- The Value of Simplification in Financial Planning
- How to Close One Chapter of Life and Open Another
- Are You and Your Partner on the Same Retirement Page?
- Retirement Mistakes to Avoid
- The Importance of Checking Your Beneficiaries
- Retirement Planning Beyond the Financials
- What's a Roth IRA?
- Great Budgeting Tips
- Do Credit Cards Have a Purpose?

Although this list only scratches the surface, it may jump-start your creative planning.

The Power of Wisdom

As you review the list, your first thought may be to focus on the knowledge you can provide. That's easy, right? You can easily talk about these topics simply by tapping into your current knowledge. But what if you dig deeper? Could you provide an extra dose of value in addition to your knowledge? What if you provided the wisdom that brings the knowledge to life?

Knowledge and wisdom are two distinct concepts that, although related, represent separate facets of human understanding. Knowledge focuses on information and facts. Wisdom, however, provides the ability to apply knowledge. While knowledge is essential, wisdom is critical to navigating life's challenges.

Why is this important? People will listen to knowledge, but they will follow wisdom. Unfortunately, we all know brilliant people who don't make wise decisions, making them hard to follow.

Let's be honest: Can you imagine your clients sitting at a cocktail party discussing the benefits of a backdoor Roth IRA or dollar cost averaging? Of course these topics are important, but most clients will struggle to share how they have changed their lives! But your clients will talk about the wisdom you share that goes beyond the numbers.

Wisdom is a blessing you can give your audience. I love this piece of wisdom from an advisor we work with. He tells his clients, "You are preparing for one retirement; we've prepared for thousands."

So, what's my point? Yes, I know clients need to know what you do. But I also think clients care as much, if not more, about who you are, and that's much easier to talk about. Sharing wisdom from your life experience can help bridge that gap. Leonardo da Vinci said, "Wisdom is the daughter of experience."

Let me share a story that illustrates a simple tip to help you bridge the gap between knowledge and wisdom in your thought leadership videos. Several years ago, I forgot this principle and learned the lesson the hard way.

The Most Important Thing

Over the years, I have had the opportunity to speak both publicly and by video often. I've learned a few tips by following great communicators and even uncovered a few of my own that have helped. I've also learned a lot from my mistakes.

On this day, I was scheduled to give a significant speech to our team. I owned a textile business at the time, and we had grown to about a hundred employees. Today was the day for me to update and encourage the troops. I had visions of this being one of those memorable speeches that someone might recall many years later. Maybe they would say it transformed their lives, and they started running marathons and climbing tall mountains! OK, I digress.

I prepared weeks in advance. I had my supporting slides ready. I had worked out my transitions. I timed everything so I would not ramble.

On the day of the speech, the team gathered in a large atrium space we had prepared just for this moment. I walked out, and then it happened.

I had forgotten the most important thing: a simple story to invite them into the conversation.

I started by saying, "Hey guys, I'm glad you are here. Today I want to provide an update." And that's when I noticed it. I saw people looking away, dropping their heads, and shifting in their seats.

I had lost them before I even started.

Why? Because after my opening line, they already felt like they knew what I would say and didn't feel they needed to listen. Sure, I had great stories later in my speech but not at the beginning.

Start with a Story

You must invite your audience into the conversation to give a great speech. And there's no better way to do that than with a story. Stories are a great way to deliver wisdom.

Here's an example: As a financial advisor, don't start your talk by saying, "Today I want to talk about social security." This screams knowledge! Instead, you might say, "Recently, I walked into my parent's home, and my mom was poring over papers. I could tell she was stressed. When I asked, she said she had been researching the best time to begin taking her social security and was more confused now than ever." This sets up a wisdom conversation.

Here's another example. Don't say, "Today I want to talk about the best time to start investing." (Knowledge) Instead, try this: "Recently, my kids had some friends over, and they were talking about their summer jobs. I heard one of them say, 'I wonder what I should do with my money. Put it in the bank? Start investing?' I quickly chimed in and shared a few benefits of saving and investing early." (Wisdom)

Here's one more. Instead of, "Today I want to talk about inflation" (Knowledge), you could say, "I was out to dinner the other night, and I overheard someone at a nearby table talking about how food prices have gone crazy." (Wisdom)

A story doesn't have to be long, maybe just a sentence or two.

For example: "I remember when I was a junior in college, and my professor said (complete the sentence)." That may be all you need. If I hear this, I at least want to know what your professor said!

One of my favorite thought leadership videos focused on wisdom came from a client who shared an interesting question he received from his young daughter. She wanted to know more about his work and asked, "Daddy, can people have too much money?" Of course, the answer to that question requires a deep dive into a wisdom bucket!

Create space for your audience to join you in the discussion. Remember, people follow wisdom. They want to join you, not listen to a lecture. So change your perspective from giving a speech to having a conversation that allows your audience to embrace the wisdom that brings your knowledge to life.

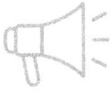

CONCLUSION

Thought leadership content is one of the foundational pillars of our strategy with clients. It is a way to deepen a relationship with a client and warm a relationship with a prospect.

Take your sales hat off for a minute and use this strategy to pour into your audience unconditionally. Soon they will put down their guard and forget it's part of your marketing plan. When that happens, they will follow you—and start sharing your content with others.

Action Steps

- Write down a list of topics that will allow you to share your wisdom in addition to your knowledge. You can start with the list in this Chapter.

- Keep a list on your desk or phone of stories you can use as illustrations to bring your knowledge to life.

- Identify the specific parts of your content that are wisdom-centered. If you are struggling, think about values. Most values are grounded in wisdom.

CHAPTER 17

HOW TO CREATE A WEBSITE THAT IS NOT AN ART MUSEUM

I want you to think about a meeting with a potential client. For this example, let's pretend it is over lunch. You arrive at the restaurant, possibly a bit early, to get a table. As your prospect approaches the table, you exchange a few pleasantries. Then, immediately, you say, "Let me tell you how great I am, how huge my business is, and all the degrees and certifications I have received in my life." Of course that's not what you say, or at least I hope not!

You probably begin the conversation by asking questions about your potential client and their family. Soon you ask about their financial challenges and possibly any anxieties or problems they have. After listening for a bit, you might share how you could help. Then, after you offer a few solutions, you begin to share about your firm and your experience.

Now, why did I give this example? Because most websites don't mirror this type of conversation. I am often amused when I look at an advisor's website only to see a huge corporate building on the main landing page. Often I want to ask, "So you must sell real estate?" Why? Because the first thing I see when I open the website is a large building. Other times I might see a chart showing the assets under management as if to say, "Look how important we are." I'm not trying to be cynical, but I'm amazed that websites don't mirror a lunch conversation with a potential client.

Not an Art Museum

If you have a website, stop now, and ask yourself, "Is my website like an art museum?" What does that mean?

It's where someone might stop and see everything you do, but there's nothing to engage them. They click on your website, scroll for a few seconds, and then leave, uninterested and not impressed. I realize your website is usually a place for someone to learn more about you, but think about it. It's still a chance to have a conversation, even if it's a digital one. If you could ask every prospect why they visited your website, most would say, "I needed help with a financial problem." I doubt they would say, "I'm a huge fan of your firm, and I wanted to read how great you are!"

So how do you create a more engaging website? Here are five simple tips you can implement today.

1) Landing Page

First, your landing page (the panel that someone lands on when they click your link) should accomplish one thing in ten seconds or less: clearly state what you do and why it benefits a potential client. Too many times, we try to get fancy or cute with these words, but they confuse the reader. Clarity trumps cute and clever every time.

For example, "We actively manage your financial portfolio so you don't have to." On the other hand, don't say, "We make your dreams come true!" Cute and clever for sure, but I don't know if you are a travel agency or Disney!

Also, the image on this panel should be a picture of smiling people. You are in a relationship business, so show that you are relatable. I often like to add B-roll video (no audio) on this panel of an advisor greeting clients, sitting with clients, smiling, and enjoying being together. Eliminate any perceptions that a visit with you is like having a root canal for your finances.

2) Questions

Second, use questions to identify the pain points. Potential clients typically check out your website for one reason. They have a problem—a pain point—and are looking for a solution. The sooner you can ask questions to uncover the paint point, the more likely they will stay on your site looking for your solution. Here are a few examples.

Do you struggle with:

- The complexities of investing your financial portfolio?

- Finding yourself too busy to devote the time needed to manage your portfolio?

- The volatility in the markets causing you to question your financial future?

- Aligning your financial plan with your dreams and goals?

- Wondering whether you will run out of money before running out of retirement?

If a prospect thinks "yes" to at least one of these questions, you now have their attention to at least continue scrolling.

3) Lead Magnet

Third, make sure you have a lead magnet that someone can download to get to know you better. For example, "The Top Five Questions You Should Ask Before Considering Retirement." Or "The Ten Most Important Things to Know About the Markets." Most people who visit your website the very first time are not ready to do business. They are often just kicking the tires. If you don't have a process that allows you to stay in touch, they may forget about you over time. A lead magnet doesn't guarantee a download, but at least it is available.

In exchange for the download, you will collect an email you can use to nurture the relationship through a prospect email campaign. Nothing salesy—start providing helpful advice that speaks to these pain points. It will keep you top of mind when a prospect is ready to take action.

4) Video

Next, about halfway down on the main page, include a video sharing your heart behind what you and your firm do to serve clients. If you clearly explain what you do on your first panel, then ask questions that lead to a yes, then offer a few examples of solutions you provide, a prospect might stop and say, "I agree so far, but what's their personality like? Will we have chemistry working together?" Remember, the purpose of this video is not to show how great you are but to explain why you do what you do. Talk about what brings you the greatest joy in serving clients.

5) Canned Photos

And finally, please, please, please, remove the canned photos. You can spot this kind of photo a mile away. It's the perfectly smiling model who looks like he or she should be on the cover of GQ or a retirement lifestyle magazine. You may have a few clients who look like this, but I suspect most don't.

Hire a photographer to shoot photos of real people. Shoot pictures of your team sitting around a table or greeting clients in your lobby. Include images of you sitting with clients in your office or conference room. Paint a picture of what it looks like to interact with your clients.

When I see canned photos, it reminds me of a few picture frames in my home that we've purchased but have yet to fill with pictures of our family.

There's no better way to be authentic than to include real people on your website. It may be the single thing that visually separates you from all the rest.

CONCLUSION

Remember, your website is a digital door to your business. Make it inviting and engaging enough for your audience to walk through. It is often the first chance to make an impression on a potential client. Your website will likely not close the sale, but it can help bridge the relationship gap. The more it mirrors a face-to-face discussion, the quicker the gap will close.

Action Steps

- If you have a current website, check whether it includes the five tips in this Chapter.

- If you don't have a website, browse a few advisor websites and scroll through as if you were a prospect. What impression did it leave? Can you spot the canned photos?

- If you want a website review, go to DiscoverBlindSpots.com/WebsiteReview, and I will send a few suggestions.

CHAPTER 18
LET'S GET REAL ABOUT SOCIAL MEDIA

I recently listened to a story from a business coach who works solely with financial advisors. This coach had started to work with a new advisor client. The firm was pretty extensive, with multiple advisors.

At one coaching session, he asked about marketing. The response to the question was surprising. The lead advisor informed the coach that they had invested more than $100,000 in social media initiatives. That raised the eyebrows of the coach to ask, "How effective has it been?" The advisor said, "I don't know." Surprised at that answer, the coach said, "I want you to look at the last twenty clients and see where they came from." A few days later, the advisor reported their findings. 90 percent of their new clients came from referrals, and any clients who came from social media were not their ideal clients. When the coach asked why they decided to pursue this strategy, the advisor said, "It seems that everyone else is doing it, so I assumed we needed to as well."

I have a friend who recently lost a family member who left him an inheritance. Until this point, he didn't see the need for the help of a financial advisor, but now he needed to develop a plan for this inheritance. I asked, "How did you find your advisor? Did you search on social media or through Google?" He said, "Heck no. I asked someone I respected for a recommendation."

It's common when I meet with a financial advisor for the challenges of social media to come up. Usually, the questions are about lack of engagement, content creation, time allocation to manage, compliance restrictions, return on investment, etc. What's interesting is the assumption that social media is the primary way to market your services. Because we spend a significant portion of our day scrolling through our phones, and because it is so accessible and easy to consume, we feel left out if we don't participate.

Now, let me clarify: I am not against social media and using it for marketing. It has its place and can provide great value. I am, however, opposed to putting all your eggs in a social media basket, especially $100,000 worth of them.

Here's where social media can help.

Billboards
Consider social media a billboard of content. As a consumer, you drive by on your phone and scroll through these billboards daily. The first billboard was introduced in 1830 by

a man named Jared Bell. P. T. Barnum saw the benefit and quickly started using the billboard strategy. Billboards have served a purpose and continue to today. But billboards are a passive way to advertise and are primarily used to create awareness of a brand. Billboards provide a message to a large audience, just like social media. But a conversation with a large audience typically doesn't produce intimate conversations. For example, I doubt a social media post is going to encourage someone to respond publicly about a financial challenge they are having. But it can be an effective tool that leads to those discussions eventually.

Another Layer

Social media platforms allow businesses to reach a larger audience to increase brand awareness. As discussed in Chapter 5, excellent communication has layers. Social media can be one of those layers, along with email, website, and print. Seeing a consistent message through multiple types of media content can increase brand awareness and credibility.

Deposit, Don't Withdraw

Don't look at social media as a cash register. Remember, you are not a transactional business, so don't use your social media solely as a sales pitch. If all your posts focus on hiring your services, you will quickly look like a late-night TV ad that says, "But wait, there's more!" A good rule of thumb is to deposit value 80 percent of the time and ask for something in return only 20 percent of the time. People will continue to follow you if they find value. On the other hand, they will unfollow you or skip over you if they feel like you always want something in return.

Consistency

Like with any marketing content, find a consistent social media rhythm and stick to it. Refrain from showing up daily only to burn out and disappear for months. Brand awareness through social media requires consistency. I know brands that post daily and others that post weekly. In the long run, consistency is more important than quantity.

Content

Usually, the biggest roadblock for social media is creating content. Work smarter, not harder, by repurposing your existing content on social media. Take sound bites from videos or blog posts; you will quickly have more content than you thought. For example, a video or blog article should produce three to five quotes each, so if you send one video or one written email a week, you may already have all the social media content you need. Also, quotes are easy content. Jot down things you say over and over to clients and post them on social media.

CONCLUSION

The best social media content can be consumed quickly and easily while scrolling. Most people are not looking for white papers to read on their social media feeds. If you think about billboards, they provide a quick message and point you somewhere. Social media can be a great tool to point people to your website to learn more.

Remember, start with the right expectation, be consistent, and deposit more than you withdraw, and social media can be an effective part of your marketing strategy.

Action Steps

- Identify the social media platforms you can use to post your content.

- Determine a sustainable rhythm. Get specific: How many times will you post a week?

- Identify longer-form content such as blog posts and videos from which you can pull your social media content.

- Keep a list of quotes you often say to clients.

- Evaluate your social media content to ensure it follows the 80/20 rule.

CHAPTER 19

A MARKETING CALENDAR TO CONSIDER

Recently I heard a leader compare the value of black and white belts in martial arts. The black belt is the pinnacle of achievement. A white belt indicates you have started the process. When this leader's martial arts instructor asked which belt he thought was most important, he said the black belt. His wise instructor informed him that he was wrong; it was the white belt. Why? Because of the significance of starting. You can't get a black belt if you sit on the sidelines.

Marketing can feel overwhelming. We often wonder where we will find the time and ability to create content and still serve clients and staff daily.

First, let's make it less overwhelming by reviewing the content ideas we have discussed.

- Written emails

- Thought leadership videos

- Quotes or short bits from your written emails or videos for social media

- Content that teaches

- Content that provides wisdom

- Next, your audience:

  - Clients

  - Prospects

- And finally, the most important, your marketing values:

  - Consistent communication deepens relationships.

  - Great marketing requires excellent communication.

  - Marketing is planting, and sales is the harvest.

  - Patience is key.

  - Slow and steady wins the race.

Whether you are a marketing ninja with a black belt or you have been standing on the sidelines wanting to try on a white belt, here are a few tips as you create your marketing calendar.

Take It in Seasons

Often, listing content ideas one by one can feel scattered. Instead, consider starting with a season or theme. For example, January-March might focus on tax prep, April-June on spring cleaning and review of your financial plan to make sure it continues to align with dreams and goals, July-September on retirement dreams and taking those fun vacations, and October-December on finishing the year well through family meetings to review your financial plan and ensure everyone is on the same page.

These themes may or may not resonate with you. If they do, great. If they don't, pick the ones that do. Focusing on a series or theme for content can help expand your creativity. Don't start with just one piece of content or one topic; look through the entire year and map out a few themes that work for your audience.

Share the Load

Most content creation will fall on your shoulders if you are the sole advisor in your office. However, empower your office staff to provide ideas. After all, they are usually on the front lines with clients, so solicit their ideas. You don't have to ask them to write the content or produce a video. However, you can ask them to jot down topics and bullets to consider.

If you have staff members who are comfortable on camera or good writers, challenge them to use those talents to help you communicate your message. For example, I once asked someone on staff to share why their firm was exceptional, and they said, "I don't feel qualified to answer this question; that should come from the advisor."

I said, "Actually, your voice might be more compelling because everyone expects the advisor to say those things."

If you have a team of advisors, assign content creation to each team member. Again, if they are comfortable on camera or are great writers, allow them to use their talents. If not, at least enlist their help in other ways to share the workload. For example, assign a quarterly theme and ask the team to map out the topics to include, with bullets for each topic.

Next, don't forget about voices from other centers of influence. For example, you can interview a CPA or an attorney to create content for your audience. After all, that's a win for both of you. They may return the favor and allow you to communicate with their audience.

Last, ask your clients. Send an email asking for topics they want you to talk about. Look for repeating themes that indicate a pain point they want you to address.

Bottom line, you don't have to sit on the sidelines feeling like you are on a deserted island. Others can help, no matter what environment you are in.

How Often?

The most important goal is to be consistent and pick a sustainable rhythm. However, the following parameters will help.

At a minimum, start communicating at least once per month. Any less and you risk confusion. In addition, your message will lose continuity if your audience wonders why they are receiving your content.

Ultimately, strive to communicate once per week. For example, I like to send emails on Tuesday, Wednesday, or Thursday and stay away from Monday and Friday. But mix it up at the beginning to find the optimal day for you and your audience. There is value in sending on a consistent day and time so your audience knows when to expect your content.

Here's a rhythm to consider.

Week 1

On the first Tuesday of the month, send a thought leadership video. It's a great way to start the month with your clients seeing and hearing from you.

Week 2

On the second Tuesday, send a different type of written content. For our financial advisor clients, we offer a voice-over that narrates an animated topic.

Week 3

On the third Tuesday, send a short message. It could be a quote from the thought leadership video you sent the first week. For our clients, we suggest sending a famous quote along with something like, "Hi John, I read this quote this morning, and it inspired me; I hope it inspires you. Have a great day!" Again, it's easy content to send that your audience might not expect, which increases the value.

Week 4

On the fourth Tuesday, take a break or use the week for more timely communication. For example, record or write a brief market update.

Repeat each month, and you will have your marketing calendar complete for the year.

CONCLUSION

Remember, don't be intimidated or overwhelmed. Jot down things you say every day, and you will be surprised at how quickly the content will come to you. If you could record every client conversation, you'd probably have enough content to fill multiple calendars. And don't worry about repeating yourself. Repetition creates consistency to reinforce the credibility of your message.

Action Steps

- Think of your content as a series or in seasons.

- Brainstorm a list of topics for each series or season with your team.

- Divide and conquer.

- Establish a sustainable rhythm.

- Plan at least three months of content at a time.

- Repeat.

CONCLUSION

If you made it to this page, thank you!

Perhaps like you, I spent years confused about how to define marketing and best use it. The plans in this book are certainly not the only way, but they are strategies that I have implemented for clients over the past years that have proved successful. Maybe not all the strategies in this book will fit you, but pick the ones that do and wear them well.

In closing, I have a few things to leave you with.

- To learn more about Discover Blind Spots and our work with financial advisors, visit DiscoverBlindSpots.com.

- If you want to identify your marketing personality, visit DiscoverBlindSpots.com/quiz.

- If you want to talk directly with me, you can reach me at tim@discoverblindspots.com.

And last but not least, I want to leave you with a gift.

A picture is worth a thousand words—if you go to the link below, you will receive access to examples of free content you are welcome to use to help you jump-start communicating a compelling message to your audience. You have a unique voice; use it!

DiscoverBlindSpots.com/FreeContent